12.3

No Need to Cook

This is not a way-out crank's cook book, a
slimmer's or even a vegetarian's cook book,
although the latter two groups should find
plenty of recipes to interest them. It is a
collection of good, tested recipes from all over
the world which do not require cooking. The
range of food we can eat raw is surprisingly
wide: fresh, dried, salted and smoked meat;
fresh, salted, pickled and smoked fish; milk,
cheeses and other dairy products, and a
multitude of salads and fruit — all these can be
prepared and eaten raw in a great number of
differing and attractive ways. By using this
book it will be easy to produce delicious,
substantial, yet nutritious meals with a
minimum amount of preparation time.

The author, Jennie Reekie, is a widely
experienced home economist and cookery
writer. Her books include *101 Dishes to Cook
the Day Before*, *Popular Cookery for Young
People*, *Fifty Super Meals for Friends and
Family*, *Traditional French Cooking* and
Casserole Cooking.

No Need to Cook

RECIPES FOR RAW FOOD

by Jennie Reekie

with illustrations by
YVONNE SKARGON

PELHAM BOOKS
LONDON

This book was designed and produced by
Park and Roche Establishment, Schaan

First published in Great Britain by
PELHAM BOOKS LTD
52 Bedford Square, London WC1B 3EF
1977

Designed by Ronald Clark
Photography by Roger Phillips
House Editor Ellen Crampton

ISBN 0 7207 1025 1

Printed in Great Britain by
Jarrold and Sons Ltd, Norwich

Contents

Introduction

This is *not* a way-out crank's cook book, a slimmer's or even a vegetarian's cook book, although the latter two groups should find plenty of recipes to interest them. It is a collection of good, tested recipes from all over the world which do not require cooking and in which none of the ingredients have ever been cooked. In an effort not to be fanatical, hot water has been permitted for peeling tomatoes, blanching peppers, and dissolving gelatine. Also, in a few recipes breadcrumbs and digestive biscuits have been used and there are some desserts using chocolate and coffee. Tabasco sauce and a can of consommé also appear a few times. Apart from these exceptions, everything is raw.

The range of food we can eat raw is surprisingly wide – meat fresh, dried, salted, and smoked; fish fresh, salted, pickled, and smoked; milk, cheeses, and other dairy products; and of course a multitude of salads and fruit – all these can be prepared and eaten raw in a great number of differing and attractive ways.

All the dishes in this book are, of course, served cold and are, therefore, ideal for summer eating, but even in winter, especially if entertaining, one can always serve cold hors d'œuvres and desserts so they may be prepared well in advance and forgotten until serving time. And also in winter we need to eat plenty of fresh raw fruit and vegetables to keep up our body's supply of Vitamin C.

Many of the original reasons for eating food raw were climatic – the Eskimos had little alternative but to eat raw caribou on their hunting trips – and drying, salting and smoking food to preserve it has been carried on for centuries by people as widely spread as the southern Africans, North American Indians, Scandinavians, and southern Europeans. Over the years some superb foods have thus evolved and in this book you will find many excellent and unusual ways of serving them.

Most of the savoury dishes can either be served on their own as hors d'œuvres or they can very happily make a main course or part of a cold buffet. By using this book it will be easy to produce delicious, substantial, yet well-balanced meals with a minimum amount of preparation time.

Not surprisingly, people are sometimes worried about the health aspect of eating raw food as cooking does, in many cases, kill any bacteria which is present. However, provided any fish or meat you eat completely raw is very fresh and you have bought it from a reliable supplier, you should not suffer any form of food poisoning. Most cured fish and meat has a very long storage life and the curing process, like cooking, will have destroyed any bacteria. Almost all the milk and cream one buys nowadays has been pasteurised, as has the cream cheese. Fruit and vegetables should, of course, always be thoroughly washed in cold water before using to remove any dirt and insects that might be present. Always make sure you dry fruit and vegetables very well before using, especially salad ingredients such as lettuce, or you will find that as soon as they are mixed with a dressing they become limp and soggy.

Fresh fruit desserts are always popular and many recipes for them can be found at the end of the book, as well as desserts using fresh cream, eggs, and cream cheese. Most of these are at their best served lightly chilled, but not so cold that the ingredients start to lose their flavour. Ice creams store well in a freezer so it saves time to make up large quantities. However, it should be packed in small containers as home-made ices need to be softened in the refrigerator before serving, and it is not advisable to soften and re-freeze a large quantity.

The number of salads one can create by blending together different vegetables, dressings, sauces, fruit, meat, fish, and cheese is endless and many readers will want to adapt some of these recipes to suit their own and their family's preferences or to what they have available at a particular time. If one wants to change an ingredient in a recipe, or alter a quantity, one can do so provided it is remembered to keep the proportions of ingredients the same. This is what has been done in the Metric and Imperial conversions shown in this book.

WEIGHTS AND MEASURES

The recipes in this book are given in Imperial and Metric weights and measures. Use only one set while making a recipe. Do not change from one to another, as they are not exact conversions – 1 oz. has been taken as 25 g and 1 pint as 500 ml (the exact conversion being 28.35 g and 567 ml).

Imperial measures

1 lb	16 oz
1 pint	20 fluid oz
¾ pint	15 fluid oz
½ pint	10 fluid oz

Metric measures

1000g	1 kg
1000ml	1 litre

FISH

IT WAS only after I had begun my research on this book that I realized just how much fish can be eaten raw, frequently without people knowing that it is in fact raw. Smoked salmon, anchovies, rollmops, all these are raw fish, although each of them has been cured in a different way. This chapter has therefore been divided into four sections, Fresh Fish (which also includes shellfish), Pickled Fish, Salt Fish, and Smoked Fish.

You will find that there are recipes literally from all over the world: Pacific Island macerated fish with lemon juice, Greek and Tunisian recipes for anchovies, a Russian recipe for smoked fish and, of course, a number of northern European recipes for salt and pickled herring, which is the fish most commonly eaten raw. Although some of these dishes could be served as a main course, most of them are best served as an hors d'œuvre.

FRESH FISH

Although some people will quite happily eat half a dozen raw oysters, for some reason they balk at the idea of eating fresh raw fish. I admit I was slightly hesitant myself but, having tried it, I was surprised to find that it did not taste fishy and had a delicate, subtle flavour. It goes without saying that if you are eating fish raw, you must be even more careful than usual about choosing really fresh fish. In Japanese restaurants you will find that they often keep the fish for Sashimi swimming about in tanks until the orders have been given, in the same way as some European restaurants keep trout and lobsters. If you are worried that the fish you have available is not as fresh as you would like, the alternative is to use frozen fish. This is generally frozen on the boats as soon as it is caught and the freezing process also helps to kill off any parasites which may be present in the fish. You should, however, use it within a few hours of defrosting.

Rather than eating plain raw fish with a sauce, in many countries, such as the West Indies and the Pacific islands, the fish is steeped in lime or lemon juice for several hours. This flavours and tenderizes the fish. It is then either served on its own, topped with a sauce, or mixed with other ingredients and you will find several different recipes for this below.

12

Mexican Mackerel
Serves 4

$1\frac{1}{2}$ lb/600g mackerel, either 1 large
   or 2 smaller fish
$\frac{1}{4}$ pint/125ml lemon juice
1 large tomato
2 oz/50g green olives
1 medium-sized onion, finely
   chopped
5 tablespoons olive oil

2 tablespoons chopped coriander
   leaves or use watercress
1 small chilli, finely chopped
good pinch salt
To garnish:
1 avocado pear
1 tablespoon lemon juice

Bone, then skin the fish, or ask the fishmonger to do this for you. Cut the mackerel flesh into $\frac{1}{2}$ inch/1.25cm cubes and put into a shallow dish. Pour over the lemon juice, cover, and leave to macerate for 2 hours, then drain off all the surplus liquid and arrange the pieces of fish on a serving dish. Peel and chop the tomato, discarding the pips, and stone the olives and chop them roughly. Put the tomato, olives, onion, olive oil, coriander or watercress, chilli, and salt into a basin. Blend well, then spoon over the fish. Peel the avocado pear and cut into slices. Dip the slices in lemon juice to preserve their colour and use them to garnish the fish.

Cuban Salmon
Serves 4

1 lb/400g fresh salmon
1 small clove garlic
salt and freshly milled black pepper

$\frac{1}{4}$ pint/125ml lemon or lime juice
To garnish:
2 tablespoons chopped parsley

Cut the salmon into $\frac{1}{2}$ inch/1.25cm cubes. Rub the cut clove of garlic all over the inside of a bowl and put in the salmon. Season with salt and pepper, then pour over the lemon or lime juice. Cover and put into the refrigerator for about 4 hours. Strain off most of the lemon juice and arrange the fish in four small dishes or in scallop shells. Sprinkle with the parsley before serving.

Kokoda
Serves 4–6

This macerated fish dish comes from the Pacific islands. The sauce for the fish is a piquant coconut cream.

$1\frac{1}{2}$ lb/600g firm white fish, such as
   tuna, halibut, or turbot
6 tablespoons lime or lemon juice
For the sauce:
2 medium-sized coconuts
grated rind and juice of 1 lemon

1 small onion, chopped
1 green chilli, finely chopped
1 teaspoon salt
$\frac{1}{4}$ pint/125ml water
To garnish:
lemon slices

Remove any bones and skin from the fish and cut it into $\frac{1}{2}$ inch/1.25cm cubes. Put into a shallow dish, pour over the lime or lemon juice, and refrigerate for 2 hours.

Crack open the coconuts, pour off the milk and grate the flesh. Put this into a bowl with the lemon rind and juice, onion, chilli, salt, and water. Mix well and squeeze out the cream with your hands, then strain through a piece of muslin. Chill while the fish is macerating. Strain off the liquid from the fish and put the fish into a serving dish or individual glasses. Pour over the coconut cream and garnish with slices of lemon.

Sashimi
Serves 4

Sashimi is a world-famous Japanese speciality and, as with other dishes, the Japanese go to enormous lengths to present it beautifully. The strips of fish are always carefully arranged on the serving plate, often in the shape of a fish, and then garnished with various leaves and flower buds. To serve the soy sauce and horseradish into which the fish is dipped before eating, you can either make up a large bowl of it or give everybody a couple of tablespoons of soy sauce in a small dish and then let them mix in as much horseradish as they like. You can use just one type of fish for the sashimi, but it will taste nicer and look more attractive if you use a mixture of fish. Tuna, sea bream, sole, smelts, cuttlefish, turbot, halibut, abalone, octopus, and squid are the most commonly used.

1 lb/400g filleted raw fish
For the sauce:
scant $\frac{1}{4}$ pint/100ml soy sauce
2 tablespoons grated horseradish

To garnish:
radishes
watercress

The fish for sashimi is generally cut into strips about $1\frac{1}{2}$ inches/3.75cm long, 1 inch/2.5cm wide, and $\frac{1}{4}$ inch/0.75cm thick, but it can be cut into 1 inch/2.5cm dice if you prefer. Arrange the sliced fish attractively on a serving plate, or put it into individual bowls and garnish simply with sliced radishes and sprigs of watercress, or more elaborately with leaves and flowers. Either stir the horseradish into the soy sauce or leave it for people to mix themselves at the table. Serve the fish as soon as possible after preparing it.

Chinese Raw Fish Strips
Serves 4

1 lb/400g plaice fillets
2 spring onions
1 tablespoon sesame or soya oil
2 tablespoons sherry

2 tablespoons soy sauce
salt and freshly milled black pepper
1 slice fresh pineapple (optional)

Skin the fish and cut into narrow strips 2 inches/5cm long. Chop the spring onions very finely and put into a shallow dish with the remaining ingredients, except the pineapple. Add the fish, toss well in the mixture and leave for 10 minutes. Lift the fish out of the mixture. Shred the pineapple very finely, if using, and mix with the fish, then arrange on a serving plate.

SHELLFISH

The oyster is the most common form of shellfish which is eaten raw but others, such as mussels, clams, cockles, and whelks can also be eaten this way. Technically it is the molluscs, as distinct from the crustaceans, i.e. crabs, lobsters, etc, which are eaten raw. Frightening stories are often passed round about the appalling food poisoning somebody's uncle had from eating oysters, and obviously there is some truth in these. The important point to remember when eating all shellfish (whether raw or cooked) is that they must be alive when you open them; you can then be certain that they are absolutely fresh. The way to tell this with molluscs having two hinged shells is this: if they are alive the shells will be tightly closed when you first look at them or, if you tap the shells or put the fish into cold water, you will see them close up almost immediately. As with all fish you should also make certain that you buy from a reputable fishmonger in a town or if you are by the sea, from a fisherman or shop which has been recommended to you.

Oysters

Oysters are found all over the world and were at one time considered to be the food of the poor but almost everywhere indiscriminate gathering from the beds has depleted stocks to such an extent that they are now a luxury. The quality and size of oysters varies a great deal, but for eating raw it is worth buying the best available, be they British oysters from Whitstable or Colchester, American oysters, or Australian oysters. The shells of the oysters should be tightly closed when you buy them (see above). Scrub the shells with a stiff brush to remove all the sand,

then hold the oyster in one hand with the flat shell up. Use an oyster knife or, alternatively, a knife with a strong, short blade. Insert the top into the hinge and twist the knife to prize the oyster open. Run the knife blade between the shells to separate them and discard the flat shell. Cut the oyster away from the shell, then replace it on the shell. When opening the oysters take care that you do not lose any of the liquor from inside the shells. The first time you try opening one it is a good idea to do it over a bowl with a sieve, so that if any of the juice is spilled you can spoon it back over the oysters. For serving, place the shells on a bed of crushed ice and lightly season the oysters with salt, pepper, and cayenne pepper, if wished. Garnish with wedges of lemon and serve brown bread and butter as an accompaniment.

Mussels

Mussels are often considered the poor man's oyster as they are inexpensive to buy and can be picked up off the rocks at low tide, but they are delicious in their own right. If you have time it is a good idea to put the mussels into a bucket of cold water, sprinkle them with oatmeal and leave them for a couple of hours. The mussels then feed off the oatmeal and excrete much of the sand and grit from the shells. Open the mussels and serve them in the same way as oysters.

Clams

Clams are readily available in the United States, and are becoming more easily available in Europe from good fishmongers. They are difficult to open but, like oysters, should be opened from the hinge with an oyster knife or a knife with a strong, short blade. Serve the clams as you would oysters.

16

Cockles, Winkles, and Whelks

These tiny shellfish can all be eaten raw. Cockles should be opened from the hinge, as oysters, although you will not need such a strong knife. Winkles and whelks need to be picked out with a pin or a very small skewer. They should also be seasoned and served with lemon.

Sea Urchins

There are several varieties of sea urchin and they are all covered with sharp spines, so you must wear stout gloves if you wish to gather them off the rocks. Cut the urchins in half with a sharp knife before serving, and serve on the half shell with lemon juice.

Shellfish Platter

A mixture of raw shellfish can be very economical to serve as you can use a minimum of the more expensive shellfish, such as oysters, together with cheaper mussels, cockles, and if you can obtain them, praires. A good mixture for each person is one oyster, two clams, about six mussels, some sea urchins (if available) and a few cockles. Open all the fish just before serving, arrange on a plate with wedges of lemon, and serve with brown bread and butter.

17

Scallops Hawaiian Style
Serves 4

1 lb/400g fresh or frozen scallops
1 onion, thinly sliced
1 tablespoon white wine vinegar
salt and freshly milled black pepper

few drops Tabasco
¼ pint/125ml fresh lime juice or use
   lemon juice

Wash the scallops and dry them well, then place in a shallow dish. Add the onion and vinegar and season with salt and pepper. Stir the Tabasco into the lime juice, pour over the scallops and toss well. Cover and refrigerate for 4 hours before serving.

Iced Clam Soup
Serves 4

10 fresh clams
½ pint/250ml single cream
¼ pint/125ml milk
1 small onion, peeled and roughly
   chopped

juice of 1 lemon
salt and freshly milled black pepper
To garnish:
few ice cubes
2 tablespoons chopped parsley

Open the clams (see page 16). Put into a blender with all the remaining ingredients and blend at high speed until smooth. Turn into a serving bowl and chill for 2 hours. Just before serving drop a few ice cubes into the bowl and sprinkle with the parsley.

PICKLED FISH

Recipes for pickled herrings abound in all northern European cooking. Scandinavia, Britain, Germany, and Holland have many versions from which to choose. Sometimes the pickled fish are served simply as they are with salad, or they are mixed with a variety of sauces and dressing. Traditionally herrings are most often

18

pickled, but there is no reason why mackerel or other oily fish, such as large sprats, cannot be used instead. If you do not want to pickle the herrings yourself, they can be bought either individually at delicatessens, or in jars in supermarkets, and these are often known as luncheon or bismark herrings.

The one recipe here for pickled fish which is not for herrings is for the famous Scandinavian Pickled Salmon with Dill. This dish is remarkably simple to prepare and the end result is really quite superb.

Pickled Herrings
For 6 herrings

6 herrings
2 oz/50g salt
1 pint/500ml water
1 large onion, finely sliced

1 pint/500ml distilled malt vinegar
1 tablespoon mixed pickling spice
1 dried chilli pepper
1 bay leaf

Clean and bone the herrings. Dissolve the salt in the water, add the herrings and leave for 2 hours. Drain, rinse in cold water, and dry well. Roll up each herring, skin side outside, with a few pieces of onion in each and pack into a wide-necked jar. While the herrings are in the brine, put the vinegar and pickling spice in a pan. Bring slowly to the boil, then remove from the heat, leave for 30 minutes, then strain and cool. Pour this cooled vinegar over the herrings in the jar and add the chilli and bay leaf. Cover the jar and leave in a cool place for 5–6 days before using the herrings, although they can be stored for several months.
Note: Although it is herrings which are traditionally pickled, other fish such as mackerel can also be treated in the same way.

German Herring Salad
Serves 6

1 pint/500ml water
1 small bay leaf
2 teaspoons chopped dill
1 onion, chopped
few white peppercorns
salt

$\frac{1}{2}$ oz/15g powdered gelatine
2 tomatoes
2 dill pickled cucumbers
2 carrots
4 pickled herrings or rollmops

Reserve 4 tablespoons water and put the remainder with the bay leaf, dill, onion, and peppercorns into a saucepan. Bring to the boil and simmer gently for 10 minutes. Season to taste with salt. Sprinkle the gelatine over the remaining 4 tablespoons water in a basin and leave to soften for 5 minutes. Stir the gelatine into the hot mixture until it has dissolved. Allow to cool, then strain. Peel the tomatoes and cut into eighths, discarding the pips. Thinly slice the cucumbers and peel and thinly slice the carrots. Cut the herrings into $\frac{1}{2}$ inch/1.25cm pieces.

Pour $\frac{1}{2}$ inch/1.25cm of the gelatine mixture into the bottom of a mould and leave until it is firmly set. Put remaining gelatine in a warm place so it will not set. Arrange the tomatoes, cucumbers, carrots, and herrings attractively in the mould and pour over the rest of the gelatine mixture. Chill the mould for 2 hours or until firm, then turn out on to a dish.

19

Herrings with Soured Cream

Many different variations of this salad are served in Scandinavia and this is a very basic recipe. Two of the most favourite additions are chopped, pickled beetroot and dill cucumbers.
Serves 4

4 rollmops or pickled herrings	salt and pepper
1 small onion	1 tablespoon chopped dill
1 dessert apple	To garnish:
2 teaspoons lemon juice	dill sprigs
$\frac{1}{4}$ pint/125ml soured cream	

Drain the herrings, cut each herring in half lengthways and then cut each half into 4 strips. Put into a basin. Slice the onion finely into rings, core and slice the apple and sprinkle it with the lemon juice. Put the onion and apple into the basin with the herrings, add the soured cream, seasoning, and dill and blend the mixture together. Turn into a serving dish and garnish with sprigs of dill before serving.

Pickled Herrings with Cheese Dressing
Serves 4

6 pickled herrings or rollmops	2 teaspoons chopped dill
4 oz/100g Bel Paese cheese	To garnish:
3 tablespoons soured cream	paprika
few drops Tabasco sauce	

Drain the herrings and cut into bite-sized pieces. If the herrings are pickled with onions, finely chop about half the onion. Mash the Bel Paese cheese in a bowl and beat in the soured cream. Add the Tabasco and dill, then stir in the herring pieces and finely chopped onion. Turn into a serving dish and sprinkle with the paprika before serving. Serve this dish within about 30 minutes of preparation as the acid in the herrings makes the dressing thicken on standing.

Orange Herring Salad
Serves 4

8 rollmops or pickled herrings	salt and freshly milled black pepper
1 lettuce heart	1 teaspoon sugar
1 large orange	3 tablespoons olive oil
$\frac{1}{2}$ teaspoon dry mustard	1 tablespoon vinegar

Drain the herrings and arrange them on a bed of crisp lettuce leaves. Thinly peel the skin from the orange. Shred the peel very finely into strips and cover with boiling water. Leave for 1 minute, then drain. Cut the orange in half and extract the juice from one half. Remove the skin and pith from the second half and slice thinly across the segments. Cut each slice into four.

Put the mustard, salt, pepper, sugar, oil, vinegar, and orange juice into a screw-topped jar. Shake well and pour over the herrings just before serving. Garnish with the strips of orange rind and the orange pieces.

◀ Orange Herring Salad and Anchovy and Tomato Salad

Gravad Lax (Pickled Salmon with Dill)
Serves 6

This Swedish dish is traditionally served at the feast on Midsummer's day.

1½ lb/600g salmon tailpiece
1 heaped tablespoon sea salt
1 heaped tablespoon granulated
  sugar
1 teaspoon black peppercorns,
  crushed
1 tablespoon brandy (optional)
1 heaped tablespoon chopped dill

For the sauce:
2 tablespoons French or German
  mustard
1 heaped tablespoon granulated
  sugar
1 large egg yolk
6 tablespoons olive oil
2 tablespoons wine vinegar
1 heaped teaspoon chopped dill
salt and freshly milled black pepper

Ask the fishmonger to fillet the fish into two triangles for you, or do this yourself. Mix the sea salt, sugar, peppercorns, brandy (if using), and dill together and spread a quarter of this over the base of a flat dish. Lay the first piece of salmon, skin side down on top of the mixture and spread half of the remaining pickle on the cut side. Place the other piece of salmon, skin side up, over the first. Rub the remainder of the pickle mixture well into the skin. Cover with foil and a board with weights on the top. Leave in a refrigerator or cold place for anything up to 5 days, but for not less than 12 hours, turning the salmon once a day. To serve, cut the salmon into slices and arrange on plates. Make the sauce by beating the mustard with the sugar and egg yolk until it is smooth. Gradually add the oil and vinegar, a teaspoon at a time, beating well. Add the chopped dill and season to taste. Serve this sauce separately as an accompaniment.

SALT FISH

Years ago fish was salted in order to preserve it, but necessity breeds a taste and the famous Herring Tables of Scandinavia would not be the same without salt herring. Anchovies also have always been salted, and even in these days of

refrigeration, you are unlikely to find fresh anchovies away from their native shores. But, however delicious these two fish are, they become quite outclassed in comparison with the third item of salt fish which is commonly eaten raw – caviar.

Caviar

Genuine Russian or Iranian Caviar from the sturgeon, and in particular the Beluga sturgeon, is prohibitively expensive. However, if you should be lucky enough to have some, it should be served simply on its own, accompanied with brown bread, which can be buttered, but the purists frown even on that. Most of us these days have to be content with substitutes such as lumpfish roe and salmon roe, but these are very good in their own right. Serve them as an hors d'œuvre with lemon wedges, finely chopped onion, and brown bread and butter.

Caviar with Cucumber
Serves 4–6

This makes an unusual and refreshing starter for a summer dinner party. Alternatively, if you cut the cucumber into smaller pieces it can be served with drinks.

1 large cucumber
4 tablespoons wine vinegar
salt
6 oz/150g cream cheese

$\frac{1}{4}$ pint/125ml soured cream
freshly milled black pepper
2 oz/50g jar caviar, or lumpfish or
  salmon roe

Peel the cucumber and cut into 1 inch/2.5cm rounds. Scoop out the centre seeds, leaving the sides and bottom to form a basket. Put on to a shallow plate. Mix the vinegar with $\frac{1}{2}$ teaspoon salt, pour over the cucumber and put into the refrigerator for at least 2 hours. Drain the cucumber and dry well. Beat the cream cheese, then beat in the soured cream. Season with salt and pepper. Spoon into the centres of the cucumber and top with the caviar, or lumpfish or salmon roe.

Caviar Dip

¼ pint/125ml soured cream
2 oz/50g jar caviar, or lumpfish or
  salmon roe

1 teaspoon Worcestershire sauce
1 tablespoon lemon juice

Blend all the ingredients together and turn the mixture into a serving bowl. Place the bowl in the centre of a large plate and surround it with suitable pieces of raw vegetable for dipping, i.e. sticks of carrot and cucumber, strips of red and green pepper, small celery sticks, radishes, cauliflower and broccoli buds, etc.

Salt Herrings

Salt herrings can be bought from good delicatessens and come in two forms, fillets and whole fish. The fillets are most common and the flavour of these will vary slightly according to the method of curing, which is often dependent on their origin, i.e. Scandinavian, Scottish, Jewish, etc. To remove the excess salt from the fillets they should be soaked in cold water or milk for 5–6 hours before using. Some delicatessens keep barrels of whole salt fish, although this is becoming increasingly rare. These herrings should first be cleaned and boned, then soaked in cold water for 12 hours. Before serving the fish should be skinned and cut into small pieces.

Matjes Herrings

These Dutch herrings are not widely available but can be found in some delicatessens. The raw fish are pickled in a light salt brine for 24 hours and, unlike salt herrings, do not require prolonged soaking before eating. The filleted fish are

24

put into brine on the boats as soon as they are caught and they are always eaten with finely chopped raw onion. They are at their best in May, when the new herring season starts, and it is a tradition that a portion of the first catch is always delivered to the palace for the Dutch Royal Family.

Pickled Salt Herrings
Serves 4

6 salt herring fillets
1 tablespoon allspice
2 bay leaves
4 oz/100g caster sugar

$\frac{1}{2}$ teaspoon black peppercorns
1 small onion, finely chopped
$\frac{1}{2}$ pint/250ml distilled malt vinegar
To garnish:
1 small onion, thinly sliced

Soak the herrings as above, then lay the fillets in a shallow dish. Mix all the remaining ingredients with the vinegar, stir until the sugar has dissolved, then pour over the fish. Cover and put into the refrigerator for at least 6 hours or overnight. Remove the herrings from the marinade, cut into narrow strips and place in a serving dish. Pour over about 6 tablespoons of the strained marinade and garnish with onion rings.

Spicy Salt Herrings
Serves 4

6 salt herring fillets
1 small onion, thinly sliced
1 small lemon, thinly sliced
1 small bay leaf

freshly milled black pepper
good pinch grated nutmeg
5 tablespoons dry cider
3 tablespoons corn or vegetable oil

Soak the herrings as above, then cut into narrow strips. Place in a serving dish with the onion and lemon. Crush the bay leaf and sprinkle over the herrings with the pepper and nutmeg. Put the cider and oil into a screw-topped jar and shake well, then pour over the herrings. Cover and chill for at least 3 hours for the flavours to infuse before serving.

Sherry Herrings
Serves 4

6 salt herring fillets
1 small onion, finely chopped
freshly milled black pepper

4 tablespoons dry sherry
To garnish:
$\frac{1}{2}$ box mustard and cress

Soak the herrings as above, then cut into narrow strips. Place in a serving dish with the finely chopped onion and sprinkle with the pepper. Pour over the sherry and garnish with the mustard and cress just before serving.

Salt Herrings in Mustard Sauce
Serves 4–6

6–8 salt herring fillets
1 leek
1 carrot
2 sticks celery
2 tablespoons French mustard

1 tablespoon sugar
salt
2 tablespoons vinegar
2 tablespoons corn oil
$\frac{1}{4}$ pint/125ml double cream

Soak the herrings as above, cut into narrow strips, and place in a serving dish. Clean the leek and cut into very thin slices. Peel the carrot and slice very thinly. Shred the celery. Scatter the vegetables over the fish. Blend the mustard, sugar, a little salt, the vinegar, and oil in a basin, then beat in the cream. Pour the sauce over the fish, cover and chill for 2–3 hours before serving.

Anchovies

Anchovies have been salted for hundreds of years because they deteriotate very rapidly when exposed to the air. The most common way of buying anchovies is canned in oil and these, if they are not very salt, or you do not mind a strong flavour in the dish, can be used as they are, or just rinsed under the cold tap to remove the excess salt. It is, however, possible to buy both anchovy fillets and whole anchovies in jars or from barrels in good delicatessens. These are generally much saltier and to remove the excess they need to be soaked in cold water or milk for about 2 hours before use. Both sorts of anchovies keep well, provided they are put into a container and covered with oil.

Anchovies Greek Style
Serves 4

10 anchovy fillets
$\frac{1}{2}$ pint/250ml water
4 tablespoons white wine
1 small onion, chopped
1 shallot, finely chopped
1 carrot, chopped
1 bouquet garni

2 teaspoons chopped thyme
1 small bay leaf
$\frac{1}{2}$ teaspoon black peppercorns
To garnish:
1 lemon
1 tablespoon chopped fennel

26

Soak the anchovy fillets in cold water or rinse them as above. Put the water, wine, onion, shallot, carrot, and bouquet garni into a saucepan. Cover, bring to the boil, and simmer gently for 30 minutes. Place the anchovy fillets in a dish with the thyme, roughly torn bay leaf, and peppercorns. Strain the hot liquid over them. Cover and leave to marinate for 24 hours. Remove the anchovies from the marinade and arrange in a serving dish together with 4 tablespoons of the marinade. Peel the lemon, discarding all the white pith, and cut into segments. Garnish the anchovies with the lemon segments and chopped fennel.

Tunisian Anchovies
Serves 3–4

18 anchovy fillets
½ teaspoon grated nutmeg

2 tablespoons finely chopped mint

Soak the anchovy fillets in cold water or rinse them as above. Dry them well. Mix the nutmeg with the mint, then roll each anchovy fillet in the mixture until it is well coated. Arrange attractively on a plate and serve with bread.

Anchovy and Tomato Salad
Serves 4

1 lb/400g tomatoes
salt and freshly milled black pepper
10 anchovy fillets

2 tablespoons olive oil
1 small clove garlic, crushed
2 oz/50g black olives

Slice the tomatoes, arrange them in a serving dish, and season with a little salt and plenty of freshly milled black pepper. Soak the anchovy fillets in cold water or rinse them as above. Dry them well, then cut into thin strips and arrange attractively on top of the tomatoes. Stone the olives, cut them in half, and scatter them on the tomatoes. Add the garlic to the olive oil and pour over the salad.

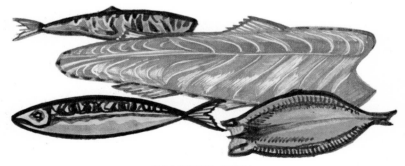

SMOKED FISH

There are two methods of smoking fish. During hot smoking the fish becomes cooked. This process is used for buckling, smoked trout, smoked mackerel, and smoked eel. Cold smoking, when the fish are smoked but the flesh is not cooked, is used for smoked salmon, kippers, smoked cod's roe, cod, haddock, etc. Haddock, cod, and kippers are generally cooked before serving but can be eaten as they are, and kippers make a very good cheap alternative to smoked salmon.

Although smoked fish can be stored for longer than fresh fish, it should be remembered that it can go mouldy. When the fish is at its best it will appear moist and with oily fish such as kippers and smoked salmon the surface will be slightly oily. It is particularly important to buy fresh smoked cod's roe, as it dries quickly and then becomes difficult to skin so that you end up having a lot of wastage.

Smoked Salmon

If smoked salmon is to be served on its own as an hors d'œuvre it must be thinly sliced. Allow 1½–2 oz/40–50g per person and arrange on individual plates. Garnish if wished with a sprig of parsley, or a sprig of fresh dill or fennel, and serve with wedges of lemon, freshly milled black pepper, and thinly sliced brown bread and butter.

Smoked Salmon with Soured Cream
Serves 4–6

For this recipe you can use smoked salmon pieces which can be bought quite cheaply from delicatessens or in packs at frozen food stores.

8 oz/200g smoked salmon	1 teaspoon French mustard
1 teaspoon black peppercorns	pinch of salt
½ teaspoon dill seed	2 tablespoons lemon juice
1 bay leaf	To garnish:
¼ pint/125ml dry white wine	1 tablespoon chopped dill
¼ pint/125ml soured cream	a few sprigs of dill

Place the salmon in a shallow dish. Sprinkle with the peppercorns and dill seed. Tear the bay leaf into several pieces, add to the dish and pour over the wine. Cover the dish tightly and leave for 8 hours or overnight in a refrigerator or cold place. Shortly before serving, remove the salmon from the marinade and place on a serving dish. Strain half the wine mixture into a basin and stir in the soured cream, mustard, salt, and lemon juice. Season with extra pepper if necessary. Pour the sauce over the salmon. Sprinkle with the chopped dill and garnish with the sprigs of dill.

Smoked Salmon Pâté
Serves 6–8

8 oz/200g smoked salmon pieces	2 teaspoons chopped dill (optional)
8 oz/200g softened butter	freshly milled black pepper
juice of 1 small lemon	salt, if necessary
4 oz/100g cream cheese	

28

Smoked Salmon Pâté ▶

Put the smoked salmon into a blender with the lemon juice and butter and blend until smooth. Add the cream cheese and dill, if used, and blend again. Season with pepper and a little salt, if necessary Turn into a serving bowl and chill for 1 hour before serving.

Smoked Cod's Roe

Peel the roe, or cut the piece of roe in half and scoop out the roe using a teaspoon. Put into a basin, mash lightly, sprinkle with a little lemon juice, and season with freshly milled black pepper. Pile onto crisp lettuce leaves on individual plates, allowing about 2 oz/50g per person. Serve with wedges of lemon and thinly sliced brown bread and butter – or with hot toast.

Taramasalata
Serves 4

As with all world-famous dishes, there are endless variations of this Greek pâté; this one is fairly simple.

4 oz/100g smoked cod's roe
1 clove garlic, crushed
2 tablespoons lemon juice

4 tablespoons olive oil
2 tablespoons cold water
freshly milled black pepper

Remove the skin from the cod's roe and discard it. Pound the roe with the garlic and lemon juice until smooth. Gradually beat in the oil and water alternately until you have a thick, smooth purée. Season to taste with pepper. Serve with bread or toast.

Smoked Cod's Roe Pâté
Serves 6

6 oz/150g smoked cod's roe
1 clove garlic, crushed
1 tablespoon lemon juice
1 tablespoon olive oil

$\frac{1}{4}$ pint/125ml double cream
freshly milled black pepper
1 tablespoon chopped parsley

Remove the skin from the cod's roe and discard it. Pound the roe with the garlic, lemon juice, and olive oil. Lightly whip the cream until it just holds its shape, then fold into the cod's roe. Turn into a serving bowl and sprinkle with the chopped parsley.

Orange Marinated Kippers
Serves 4

2 tablespoons corn or vegetable oil
grated rind and juice 1 orange
6 black peppercorns

3 small bay leaves
6–8 kipper fillets

Put the oil, orange (rind and juice), peppercorns, and bay leaves into a screw-topped jar and shake well. Skin the kipper fillets and lay them in a shallow dish. Pour over the orange marinade, cover and leave in the refrigerator for 12–24 hours. Arrange the kipper fillets in a serving dish, strain over the marinade and serve with a tossed green salad.

Simple Kipper Pâté
Serves 6–8

8 oz/200g kipper fillets
4 tablespoons white wine
8 oz/200g softened butter

1 small clove garlic, crushed
 (optional)
freshly milled black pepper

Skin the kipper fillets and place in a shallow dish. Pour over the wine, cover and marinate in the refrigerator for 12 hours. Put the kipper fillets into a blender, or pound them well, then add the butter, garlic if used, and pepper to taste. Spoon into a serving dish and chill for at least 1 hour.

Kipper Salad with Horseradish
Serves 4

6–8 kipper fillets
4 tablespoons lemon juice
2 dessert apples

2 tablespoons horseradish sauce
To garnish:
$\frac{1}{2}$ box mustard and cress

Skin the fillets and cut them into thin strips. Put into a shallow dish, pour over the lemon juice and leave for 2 hours. Core the apples, peel them if liked, but they can be left unpeeled, and add to the kippers, then stir in the horseradish sauce. Mix well, turn into a serving dish and garnish with mustard and cress.

Kippers in Curry Mayonnaise
Serves 4

8 kipper fillets
3 tablespoons lemon juice
1 dessert apple
4 tablespoons mayonnaise
2 teaspoons mild curry powder

2 sticks celery, chopped
To garnish:
few lettuce leaves
4 slices lemon

Skin the kipper fillets, cut them into strips and put them into a shallow dish. Pour over the lemon juice and leave to marinate for 2 hours. Core the apple, peel if wished, and dice. Add to the kippers and toss lightly together so that the apple is coated with lemon juice. Stir the curry powder into the mayonnaise and blend well. Add the kipper, apple, and celery and toss together. Place a couple of crisp lettuce leaves on each of four individual serving plates and divide the kipper mixture among them. Garnish with twists of lemon.

Russian Cold-Smoked Fish Salad
Serves 4

12 oz/300g smoked cod or haddock
2 tablespoons French mustard
4 tablespoons oil
freshly milled black pepper

1 medium-sized onion, very thinly
  sliced
1 tablespoon chopped parsley

Skin the fish and cut into thin slices. Put the mustard into a basin and gradually beat in the oil. Season with pepper and stir in the onion and fish. Turn into a serving dish, cover and refrigerate for 2–3 hours. Sprinkle with the parsley before serving.

MEAT

FRESH MEAT

Ancient man for generations ate his meat raw like the animals; then he discovered fire and the art of cooking. While the endless variations which can be achieved by cooking meat obviously make this a preferable way of eating it most of the time, raw meat, especially if it is lightly chilled in hot weather, makes a very pleasant change. Use only tender, lean meat and, unless you are using fillet steak, put it through a mincer a couple of times to break down the fibres. Beef is the meat most commonly eaten raw, although lean lamb cut from the leg can also be used. It is not advisable to eat raw pork as it goes off very quickly and can also contain parasites.

The three recipes given here can all be varied according to individual taste. For example, instead of stuffing peppers, you could stuff large tomatoes, or you could add some crushed garlic and/or soy sauce instead of the Worcestershire sauce to the meat mixture. Steak tartare is a classic dish, but this can be varied by using mayonnaise with a few drops of Tabasco instead of tartare sauce, by adding chopped chives instead of – or as well as – parsley. Always season the meat well with plenty of salt, preferably sea salt, and freshly milled black pepper.

34

Steak Tartare
Serves 1

This must surely be the most famous of all raw dishes. Some people hate the idea of it, even though they will eat rare roast beef or a rare steak, but having tried it once it is easy to become addicted.

4 oz/100g good quality fillet steak, rump steak, or topside
salt and freshly milled black pepper
1 egg yolk
1 small onion, finely chopped
1 tablespoon chopped capers
½ green or red pepper, finely chopped
2 teaspoons chopped parsley
2 tablespoons tartare sauce (see page 48)

Finely mince the meat and season with salt and pepper. Form into a flat cake and place in the centre of a dinner plate. Make a shallow hollow in the centre of the steak and place the egg yolk in it, if you wish this can be left in half the shell. Arrange the onion, capers, peppers, parsley, and tartare sauce neatly in mounds round the outside of the steak. Cover and chill. To serve, mix the seasonings thoroughly into the meat and egg yolk, using a knife and fork.

Stuffed Peppers Tartare
Serves 4

4 medium-sized green peppers
1 lb/400g good quality fillet steak, rump steak, or topside
2 egg yolks
1 tablespoon chopped gherkins
1 tablespoon chopped onion (optional)
1 tablespoon Worcestershire sauce
1 teaspoon French mustard
salt and freshly milled black pepper

Slice the tops off the peppers and remove the cores and seeds. Finely mince the steak, then add the egg yolks, gherkins, onion, if used, Worcestershire sauce, and mustard and season to taste with salt and pepper. Spoon the mixture into the pepper cases and top with the pepper lids. Chill for 1 hour before serving. Serve with mayonnaise and a tomato salad.

Curried Lamb
Serves 4

1 lb/400g lean lamb cut from the leg
2 large tomatoes
4 heaped tablespoons mayonnaise
1 tablespoon curry powder
1 tablespoon finely chopped onion
1 clove garlic, crushed
salt and freshly milled black pepper
To garnish:
crisp lettuce leaves
sprigs of watercress

Finely mince the lamb and put into a bowl. Peel the tomatoes and chop finely, discarding the seeds. Add to the meat with the mayonnaise, curry powder, onion, garlic, and seasoning. Blend well. Pile into four mounds on individual dinner plates and garnish with crisp lettuce leaves and sprigs of watercress.

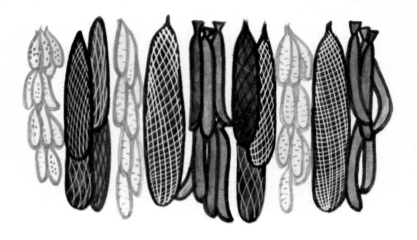

DRIED, SALTED, AND SMOKED MEATS

I have put all these meats under one heading as the majority of the meats which are dried are salted and they are very often smoked as well. The most common form of dried meat is salami or, as the French call it, *saucisson sec*. All these words, including sausage, stem from the Latin words *salsus* – meaning salted – and *salsicia*, something prepared by salting. The Romans were the first known sausage makers and as the name implies, it was meat (generally pork, although other meats such as beef and goat were used) which was salted to preserve it for consumption during the winter months when food was scarce.

Another form of raw salted meat which is readily available is Continental ham, such as Italian Parma, French Bayonne, and Morvan and German Westphalia ham, and it is also possible to buy some locally cured hams in charcuteries in country villages throughout Europe. All these hams are cured in brine, then generally smoked and left to mature to give them their traditional flavour and they are served raw in very thin slices.

The idea of smoked sausages and hams hanging from the farmhouse kitchen is romantic, but even in country areas very little is still done in the home. One of the biggest problems these days is obtaining the necessary quantities of small or large intestine to put the sausage into. It is also important to keep the drying temperature steady and in modern, centrally heated houses this is not very easy. However, for those who would like to explore this subject further, I would suggest reading Jane Grigson's *Charcuterie and French Pork Cookery*, published by Michael Joseph and Penguin Books.

Most forms of dried meat are highly nutritious as the nutrients in the meat are concentrated with the weight loss that occurs. For this reason various forms of dried meat have been used all over the world for centuries by people going on long hunting expeditions or to war, so that the amount they had to carry was reduced to the minimum. Biltong, which comes from southern Africa, is strips of meat which are either sun dried or hung from the rafters of a high, draughty shed and left until they become like leather. It is then eaten either grated or cut into very thin pieces and the best biltong is supposed to be that of the ostrich. The North American Indians made Pemmican from dried meat, usually venison or buffalo, which was dried in the same way as biltong. After drying the meat was ground down and mixed with an equal quantity of fat and some raw berries or cherries. It was then formed into cakes which were packed tightly into rawhide bags to preserve them. Early settlers copied this idea, often using beef and raisins, and a similar mixture was made up to take on some of the very early Arctic explorations. In Europe there are various kinds of dried meat of which the Swiss Bundnerfleisch and Italian Brasaola are the most famous, but very few of these are exported and they are always very expensive. However, if you are lucky enough to find some they are worth trying as most of them are quite delicious.

Parma Ham with Melon

This is a classic Italian dish. You can either simply cover individual plates with very thinly sliced Parma ham and top it with slices of ripe, lightly chilled melon, or you can wrap slices of ham round thin wedges of melon and secure them with a cocktail stick. Alternatively, cut the melon into large cubes, wrap pieces of ham around them, and serve.

Parma Ham with Figs
Serves 4

8 medium-sized figs
4 oz/100g cream cheese
3 tablespoons mayonnaise
salt and freshly milled black pepper

pinch cayenne pepper
4 oz/100g thinly sliced smoked raw
ham

Using a sharp knife, cut each fig almost in half lengthways, but stop about ½ inch/1.25cm from the bottom to give you a hinge. Sieve the cream cheese, then stir in the mayonnaise and season to taste with salt, black pepper, and cayenne pepper. Put a good teaspoonful of this filling in the cut of each fig. Cut the ham into thin strips and wrap them round the bottom of the figs, securing each one with a cocktail stick, then arrange on a serving dish.
Note: For an easy starter, simply arrange slices of Parma ham on individual plates and place figs, cut into halves or quarters, on top.

Westphalia Ham with Cucumber
Serves 4

1 small onion, finely chopped
½ small cucumber, peeled and
   grated
salt
4 tablespoons oilve oil
2 tablespoons white wine vinegar

1 tablespoon chopped parsley
freshly milled black pepper
4 oz/100g Westphalia or other thinly
   sliced smoked raw ham
To garnish:
1 red or green pepper, sliced

Put the onion and cucumber into a sieve, sprinkle with a little salt and leave for 30 minutes to drain. Dry well. Put the oil, vinegar, parsley and seasoning into a screw-topped jar and shake well. Blend 1 tablespoon of this with the cucumber and onion. Lay the slices of ham flat on a board and divide the cucumber mixture between them. Roll the ham up neatly and place in a serving dish. Pour over the remaining dressing and leave to marinate for 3 hours. Garnish with the pepper before serving.

Italian Meat Antipasto

A typical starter to many Italian meals is a plate of dried and smoked meats, usually consisting of salami of various kinds, brasaola, slices of mortadella, and a little Parma ham. In Italy the meats are literally sliced wafer thin, and it is worth while insisting that your delicatessen does the same, as not only does it make the meat go much further, but you also seem to be better able to taste the full flavour of each slice of meat. The meat should be attractively arranged on a large serving plate or on individual plates. Allow about 2 oz/50g meat per person for a starter, provided it is thinly sliced. The meat can be garnished with sprigs of parsley, slices of onion and/or small wedges of lemon. Serve with plenty of fresh French bread or with buttered rye bread.

Pomodori con Proscuitto (Tomatoes with Proscuitto)

Ideally you should use Parma ham for this recipe, but other raw hams, such as Morvan, Westphalia, and Bayonne could be used if you find these more readily available. I have made the quantity of ham adjustable so that you can fit it in with your purse!

4 medium-sized tomatoes
salt and freshly milled black pepper
2 teaspoons chopped basil
2–4 oz/50–100g raw ham
2 teaspoons chopped capers

1 teaspoon finely chopped onion
4 tablespoons mayonnaise
To garnish:
parsley sprigs

Cut off the tops from the tomatoes and scoop out the insides. Stand them upside down and leave to drain for 30 minutes. Season the insides of the cases with salt and pepper and sprinkle with the basil. Chop the ham finely and put into the bottom of the tomato cases. Add the capers and onion to the mayonnaise and

38

Italian Meat Antipasto ▶

spoon into the tomatoes on top of the ham. Garnish with a sprig of parsley and chill for 1 hour before serving, if possible.

Variation: Put 1 teaspoon finely chopped celery into the bottom of each tomato with the ham.

Genoese Salad
Serves 1

2 oz/50g salami, thinly sliced
1 oz/25g cream cheese
1 stick celery, finely chopped

salt and freshly milled black pepper
4 black olives.

Arrange the salami in a circle on a small plate. Put the cream cheese into a basin, stir in the celery, and season to taste with salt and pepper. Spoon the cream cheese mixture into the centre of the plate and garnish with the olives.

Stuffed Salami Cornets
Serves 4–6

16 thin slices large salami
8 oz/200g cream cheese
3 tablespoons single cream
1 clove garlic, crushed
1 tablespoon very finely chopped
   basil

salt and freshly milled black pepper
To garnish:
crisp lettuce leaves
8 large black olives

Remove the skin from the salami and make a cut into the centre of each slice, then roll the salami round to form a cornet. Beat the cheese with the cream, then beat in the garlic, basil, and seasoning. Put the mixture into a piping bag fitted with a large rose pipe and pipe the cream cheese mixture into the salami cornets. Arrange on a serving plate with the lettuce leaves. Halve the olives and remove the stones. To garnish place half an olive on the point of each rosette of cream cheese.

Salami and Tomato Antipasto
Serves 4

4 oz/100g thinly sliced salami
4 oz/100g Bel Paese or Provolone
   cheese, diced
4 large tomatoes
2 oz/50g black olives
1 red pepper

2 tablespoons finely chopped
   parsley
1 tablespoon olive oil
2 teaspoons lemon juice
salt and freshly milled black pepper

Arrange the salami on a serving plate. Dice the cheese, peel and slice the tomatoes, and arrange them on the plate with the olives. Finely shred the red pepper, discarding the core and seeds, and put into a basin with the parsley. Add the oil, lemon juice, and seasoning and toss the ingredients to mix them. Pile into the centre of the serving plate.

Salami in French Dressing
Serves 4

8 oz/200g sliced, well-flavoured
   salami or garlic sausage
4 tablespoons olive oil
¼ teaspoon coriander seed, crushed

1 tablespoon finely chopped onion
2 teaspoons finely chopped capers
2 tablespoons chopped parsley
salt and freshly milled black pepper

Arrange the salami in a shallow dish. Mix the oil with the coriander, onion, capers, parsley, and seasoning. Spoon over the salami or garlic sausage and leave to marinate for 8 hours before serving.

Salami and Olive Salad
Serves 4

4 oz/100g thinly sliced salami
4 oz/100g black olives
1 tablespoon very finely chopped
   onion

2 tablespoons olive oil
2 teaspoons vinegar
1 teaspoon coriander seeds, crushed
1 teaspoon finely chopped basil

Arrange the slices of salami round the outside of a serving plate. Stone the olives and put into a basin with the onion, oil, vinegar and coriander seeds. Toss well together and place in the centre of the serving dish. Sprinkle with the basil just before serving.

Fennel Salad with Mortadella
Serves 4

4 Florence fennel roots
5 tablespoons mayonnaise
3 tablespoons single cream
1 teaspoon chopped capers

1 teaspoon paprika
4 oz/100g mortadella
salt and freshly milled black pepper
2 tablespoons chopped parsley

Wash the fennel roots and discard any tough outside leaves. Cut each fennel root into four and arrange in the bottom of a shallow serving dish. Blend the mayonnaise, cream, capers, and paprika in a basin. Chop the mortadella into ¼ inch/0.75cm pieces and add to the mayonnaise. Taste and adjust the seasoning, then spoon over the fennel and sprinkle with the chopped parsley.

Mortadella rolls
Serves 4

2 oz/50g Ricotta or other cream
   cheese
4 heaped tablespoons mayonnaise
½ bunch watercress, finely chopped
1 small onion, finely chopped
1 teaspoon chopped capers

1 teaspoon French mustard
8 thin slices mortadella
To garnish:
1 tablespoon thick mayonnaise
8 onion rings

41

Mash the cheese, then blend in the mayonnaise. Stir in the watercress, onion, capers, and mustard. Blend well. Divide this stuffing among the slices of mortadella, then roll each one up into a cylinder and place on a serving dish. To garnish, pipe a rosette of mayonnaise on each roll and arrange a ring of onion on top.

EGGS

I SHALL NEVER forget my feeling of horror when a Swiss friend came down for breakfast, took an egg out of the refrigerator, made a small hole in the bottom with a skewer, and proceeded to suck out the contents. I could think of nothing more revolting, but she assured me that, as far as she was concerned, it was the only way to eat an egg. In fact my revulsion was quite illogical as I quite happily eat mayonnaise with raw egg yolk, mousses with raw egg whites, or drink an egg flip. Raw eggs are supposed to be very good for you and, although I still do not like the idea of tackling a Prairie Oyster, I have given the recipe for those who do.

There are innumerable different egg- and oil-based sauces, of which mayonnaise is obviously the most well known. This, of course, blends well with all salads, but Tartare Sauce, traditionally served with fried fish, is also very good with fish, meat, and vegetable salads. A bowl of Aioli or Skordalia served with plenty of crisp, fresh vegetables, such as carrots, celery, cucumber, radishes, peppers, etc, makes a very pleasant summer appetizer. If you are worried about being unpopular the following day, a useful tip for helping to remove the smell of garlic on your breath is to eat a small bunch of raw parsley. This is also extremely good for you as parsley has a very high Vitamin C content and helps clear the blood.

One word of warning about eating raw eggs: there is nothing the matter with eating hens' or bantams' eggs, providing of course they are fresh, but it is not advisable to eat raw duck or goose eggs as the pores in the shell allow air and, consequently, bacteria to enter.

SAVOURY RECIPES AND SAUCES

Prairie Oyster

The story of the origin of the Prairie Oyster is that a member of a hunting party became ill on the Texas prairies and developed a craving for oysters. Hardly surprisingly, there were none available for hundreds of miles, so another member of the party broke some hens' eggs into a glass with a teaspoonful of vinegar and sprinkled them with some freshly milled black pepper and a little salt. The invalid took it and recovered! I don't imagine it is the cure of all ills, but devotees swear it does them a lot of good. If you prefer, you can replace the vinegar with a few drops of Worcestershire sauce.

Anchovy Eye
Serves 1

This is one of the very characteristic dishes of the Swedish smörgasbord.

8 anchovy fillets
1 onion, finely chopped

2 teaspoons chopped parsley
1 large egg yolk

Soak the anchovy fillets in cold water for 2 hours if they are very salt. If not, rinse them under a cold tap to remove the excess salt. Drain them well, then chop finely and arrange in a ring round the edge of a small plate. Put a ring of chopped onion inside them and sprinkle this with the chopped parsley, then place the raw egg yolk carefully in the centre.

Mayonnaise
Makes $\frac{1}{2}$ pint/250ml

For cold cookery mayonnaise is just as important as a good French dressing. Although it is possible to buy excellent proprietary brands, none of these really

quite matches up to the flavour of home-made, which is generally cheaper as well. To make mayonnaise with olive oil is extremely expensive, so I generally use corn oil, good quality vegetable oil, or – if I particularly want the mayonnaise to have a Mediterranean flavour to it – one third to one half olive oil and the remainder corn oil. To obtain the best results, all the ingredients should be at room temperature when you start as this minimizes the risk of curdling. Should the mayonnaise curdle however, do not despair, simply break a fresh egg yolk into a clean basin and beat in the curdled mixture a teaspoon at a time. Mayonnaise will keep very satisfactorily for a couple of weeks in a covered container in the refrigerator, but store it in the warmest part because if it gets too cold and freezes it will separate out and curdle, in which case treat as above.

2 egg yolks
salt and freshly milled black pepper
½ teaspoon French mustard

2 tablespoons wine vinegar
½ pint/250ml oil (see above)

Put the egg yolks, seasoning, mustard, and 1 tablespoon of the vinegar into a basin. Using either a wooden spoon or a balloon whisk, whichever you find easier, mix until they are well blended. Beat in the oil gradually, drop by drop until you have added about half of it and the mixture is beginning to look thick and shiny, then beat in the remainder of the oil a little more quickly. When all the oil has been incorporated, beat in the remaining vinegar. Taste and adjust seasoning.

Blender Mayonnaise

If you make mayonnaise in a blender it is possible to use a whole egg rather than 2 egg yolks, as the rapid whisking of the beaters makes a smooth emulsion with the oil, although the sauce tends to be softer than if made by the traditional method with egg yolks only.

Break one egg into the blender and add all the vinegar, the seasoning, and the mustard, as above. Switch the blender to high speed and mix well. If your blender has a hole in the lid, use this to pour the oil through, if it does not it is worthwhile making a temporary lid out of foil and making a hole in this. Keep the blender at high speed and pour in the oil in a slow, steady stream until it has all been incorporated and the sauce is thick and smooth.

Aioli (French Garlic Mayonnaise)
Makes ½ pint/250ml

This sauce is sometimes described as the 'Butter of Provence'. Serve with salads in place of mayonnaise or see page 44.

3–4 cloves garlic, crushed
2 egg yolks
salt and freshly milled black pepper

½ pint/250ml oil (this should be all olive but you can use half olive and half corn oil)

Put the garlic into a basin, add the egg yolks and seasoning and beat well, then add the oil gradually as if making mayonnaise above.

Skordalia (Greek Garlic Mayonnaise)
Makes scant $\frac{1}{2}$ pint/200ml

Technically this sauce is not raw, as breadcrumbs are incorporated into it, but I felt it was worth including as it is excellent served with fresh raw vegetables.

4 cloves garlic, crushed
1 egg yolk
salt and freshly milled black pepper
$\frac{1}{4}$ pint/125ml oil, preferably olive

2 oz/50g fresh white breadcrumbs
2 oz/50g ground almonds
1 tablespoon lemon juice
2 tablespoons chopped parsley

Put the garlic into a basin, add the egg yolk and seasoning and beat well. Gradually add the oil a drop at a time, as for mayonnaise above. When all the oil has been incorporated, stir in the breadcrumbs and the almonds, then the lemon juice and parsley. Taste and adjust the seasoning before serving.

Rémoulade Sauce
Makes $\frac{1}{2}$ pint/250ml

Rémoulade Sauce is the classic accompaniment to grilled and fried meat, but can be served with any salad and is used for Celery Rémoulade (page 77).

$\frac{1}{2}$ pint/250ml mayonnaise
2 teaspoons French mustard
2 teaspoons finely chopped capers

1 teaspoon chopped parsley
1 teaspoon chopped tarragon
1 teaspoon chopped chervil

Put the mayonnaise into a basin, blend in all the remaining ingredients, and leave the sauce for the flavours to infuse for at least 30 minutes before using.

Tartare Sauce
Makes $\frac{1}{2}$ pint/250ml

$\frac{1}{2}$ pint/250ml mayonnaise
1 tablespoon chopped parsley
1 tablespoon chopped capers

1 tablespoon finely chopped
  gherkins
1 tablespoon whipped double cream
  (optional)

Put the mayonnaise into a basin, blend in all the remaining ingredients, including the cream if using. Leave the sauce for at least 30 minutes for the flavours to infuse before using.

DRINKS

Orange Egg Flip
Serves 1

juice of 3 medium-sized oranges
1 egg

1 tablespoon honey

Put all the ingredients into a blender and mix until smooth and frothy. Pour over cracked ice in a glass and serve at once.

Iced Banana Flip
Serves 1

1 banana
½ pint/250ml iced milk
2 teaspoons malt extract (optional)

2 teaspoons honey
1 egg
little grated nutmeg

Peel and roughly chop the banana and put it into a blender with the milk, malt extract, honey, and egg. Blend until smooth and frothy, then pour into a glass and sprinkle with the nutmeg. Serve at once.

Port Flip
Serves 4

scant ½ pint/200ml port
2 eggs
2 teaspoons caster sugar

2 tablespoons Bénédictine
¾ pint/375ml crushed ice
grated nutmeg

Put the port, eggs, sugar, Bénédictine and ice into a blender. Blend for 1 minute, then pour into 4 glasses and serve sprinkled with nutmeg.

DESSERTS

Chocolate Mousse
Serves 4

This must be one of the simplest and most popular of all desserts. It can be varied in an enormous number of ways. You can add the grated rind and juice of a small orange to the chocolate mixture, or a couple of teaspoons of instant coffee, or a couple of tablespoons of rum or brandy. If you wish you can also add ¼ pint/125ml of whipped cream before folding in the egg whites.

4 oz/100g plain chocolate
1 tablespoon unsalted butter

3 large eggs, separated

Put the chocolate, broken into small pieces, into a basin over a pan of hot water. Leave until the chocolate has melted, then remove from the heat and beat in the butter and egg yolks. Whisk the egg whites until they form soft peaks, then fold into the chocolate mixture. Divide among four small dishes and leave for at least 30 minutes to set.

Lemon Whip
Serves 4

¼ pint/125ml cold water
4 oz/100g caster sugar
½ oz/15g powdered gelatine
finely grated rind and juice of
   2 lemons

2 egg whites
To decorate:
2 tablespoons chopped walnuts

Pour the water into a basin, add the sugar and stir well, then sprinkle over the gelatine. Leave to soften for 5 minutes. Stand the basin over a pan of hot water and leave until the sugar and gelatine have dissolved. Remove from the heat and stir in the lemon rind and juice. Stand the mixture in a cool place and leave until it is beginning to thicken, then whisk until it is light and frothy. Stiffly whisk the egg whites and fold into the lemon mixture. Spoon into a serving dish and leave in a cool place until set. Sprinkle with the chopped walnuts before serving.

DAIRY PRODUCE

MILK IS OFTEN described as the most natural food of all and certainly it is the most complete, containing fat, protein, carbohydrate, calcium, and Vitamins A, B and D. This chapter deals with milk and its products, cream, cheese, and yogurt – from which some of the quickest and simplest, but most delicious meals can be created.

MILK

Milk shakes

To flavour milk shakes you can use specially prepared powders and syrups, fresh fruit, or fruit purées. To ½ pint/250ml milk allow ½ large banana or 2 tablespoons fresh raspberry, strawberry, or blackcurrant purée and sweeten to taste with sugar.

Slimmer's Cocktail (A milk and egg diet)

This is a diet which was given to my mother years ago. If you follow it for 3 days you should lose at least 4 lb/1.75 kilo or up to 7 lb/3.25 kilo. Make up the amount of cocktail given below and have a glass for breakfast, lunch, and supper or, if you prefer, have smaller glasses and include one for tea. Eat or drink nothing else. Always remember though, that diets are for healthy people, so if you have any doubts first consult your doctor.

2 eggs
juice of 2 large oranges

1 tablespoon corn or vegetable oil
1 pint/500ml cold milk

Either whisk all the ingredients together or put them into a blender and blend until frothy. Keep in the refrigerator during the day as the mixture is best well chilled.

52

Devonshire Junket

Serves 4–6

The increased popularity of yogurt and other milk- and cream-based desserts has resulted in junket going into a decline and to many people it is thought of as a rather unpleasant watery pudding they had in their childhood. However, a well-made, old-fashioned junket is delicious and well worth trying. The addition of brandy makes this a strictly adult dessert.

1 pint/500ml full cream milk
2 teaspoons sugar
2 tablespoons brandy
1 teaspoon rennet

4 oz/100g clotted cream
¼ teaspoon ground cinnamon or
    grated nutmeg

Put the milk into a saucepan and bring just to blood heat. Mix the sugar and brandy in a serving bowl, add the warmed milk, then stir in the rennet. Cover the bowl and leave to set in a warm place for about 3 hours. When set, spread the cream over the top of the junket and sprinkle with the cinnamon or nutmeg. If you find the clotted cream is too thick to spread, soften it with a little fresh cream or top of the milk.

YOGURT

Like cheese, yogurt has been made for centuries and in many civilizations there are innumerable legends surrounding its healing properties. In the Balkans, where it is eaten extensively, they say it is responsible for longevity, and no one has so far been able to dispute this!

The simplest way to eat it is on its own with sugar, honey, or fresh fruit, but it can be used in all sorts of savoury and sweet dishes, sauces, and dressings.

In recent years there has been an enormous growth in the commercially made yogurt market, and, as well as natural yogurt, it is now possible to buy a wide range of fruit and other flavoured yogurts. Most of this yogurt is low fat, which is of special value to slimmers, as it is made from the skimmed milk left after making butter and cream. You will, however, find it much cheaper to make your own yogurt and there are a number of yogurt-making machines on the market. These, however, are not essential, provided you have a suitable warm place to leave the yogurt to set, such as a warm airing cupboard, the back of an Aga or other solid fuel cooker, or even beside a pilot light on a gas cooker.

To Make Yogurt

All yogurt is alive and contains a bacillus, so you must have some natural yogurt in order to start making your own. Bring 1 pint/500ml of milk (either whole milk or skimmed milk) slowly up to boiling point, then remove from the heat. When it has cooled to blood temperature, stir in 3 tablespoons of natural yogurt and blend it really well: do not add the yogurt when the milk is still very hot as this will kill the bacillus. Pour the milk into individual pots, cover and put into a warm place (see above). Leave for 8–12 hours or until the yogurt has set, then put into the refrigerator to chill. It will keep well for several days. Once you have started the chain, always remember to keep back 3 tablespoons of yogurt for making the next batch.

Jeryik (Greek hors d'œuvre)
Serves 4

4 tablespoons finely diced cucumber
good pinch salt
½ pint/250ml natural yogurt

2 cloves garlic, crushed
2 tablespoons chopped parsley
freshly milled black pepper

Put the cucumber into a colander, sprinkle with the salt and leave to drain for 30 minutes. Stir into the yogurt with the remaining ingredients and leave to infuse for 15 minutes before serving. Serve with pitta or French bread.

Yogurt and Chive Dressing
Serves 4

This is an ideal slimmer's dressing to serve with a green salad.

¼ pint/125ml natural yogurt
1 tablespoon chopped chives

1 teaspoon French mustard
salt and freshly milled black pepper

Turn the yogurt into a basin, then blend in the remaining ingredients. Leave for 30 minutes for the flavours to infuse before serving.

Danish Blue Dressing
Serves 4

This dressing can be used with any salad, but blends particularly well with any containing tomato and crisp lettuce.

¼ pint/125ml natural yogurt
2 oz/50g Danish Blue cheese, crumbled

salt and freshly milled black pepper

Turn the yogurt into a basin, then crumble in the cheese and season to taste with salt and pepper. This dressing will keep for several days in a covered container in the refrigerator.

Natural Wonder Soup
Serves 4

½ pint/250ml natural yogurt
1 pint/500ml tomato juice
1 tablespoon Worcestershire sauce
¼ cucumber, finely chopped

salt and freshly milled black pepper
To garnish:
1 tablespoon chopped chives

54

Natural Wonder Soup ▶

Lightly whisk the yogurt and tomato juice together. Add the Worcestershire sauce and cucumber and season to taste. Chill for at least 3 hours and serve garnished with chopped chives.

Dutch Yogurt Pudding
Serves 4–6

4 tablespoons water
½ oz/15g powdered gelatine
1 pint/500ml natural yogurt
juice of ½ lemon

2 oz/50g caster sugar
2 tablespoons sultanas
2 tablespoons chopped glacé
   cherries

Put the water into a basin, sprinkle over the gelatine and leave to soften for 5 minutes. Stand the basin over a pan of gently simmering water and leave until the gelatine has dissolved, then remove from the heat. Tip the yogurt into a bowl, stir in the gelatine, lemon juice, sugar, sultanas, and cherries and blend well. Turn into a serving dish and leave in the refrigerator until set. Serve the dessert with fresh whipped cream, if desired.

Sweet Yogurt Dressing
Serves 4

Serve this poured over fresh fruit, such as strawberries or apples.

¼ pint/125ml natural yogurt
2 teaspoons clear honey

good pinch powdered cinnamon

Blend all the ingredients together and chill lightly before serving.

Orange and Yogurt Cup
Serves 1

This makes a refreshing and nutritious drink – ideal for breakfast or a quick lunch.

¼ pint/125ml natural yogurt
juice of 1 large orange

1 egg

Either put all the ingredients into a blender and blend until smooth or whisk all the ingredients together in a bowl.

CREAM

Cream – I always feel – is one of the luxuries of life: one can manage perfectly well without it, but it subtly improves everything to which it is added, often changing it from something ordinary into something quite *extra*ordinary. With a pot of double cream in the refrigerator you will never find it difficult to make a delicious dessert in a matter of minutes.

Soured cream, which is used extensively in Russian, Austrian, and Hungarian cookery, has a pleasant, refreshing tang to it. If you find it difficult to buy commercially soured cream, you can sour double cream by adding a tablespoonful of lemon juice to it.

Austrian Soured Cream Dressing
Serves 6

Serve with fish salads or use in place of mayonnaise in Coleslaw (page 73).

1 egg yolk
2 tablespoons wine vinegar
$\frac{1}{2}$ pint/250ml soured cream

1 tablespoon chopped chives or
   spring onions
freshly milled black pepper

Blend the egg yolk, then beat in the vinegar. Stir in the cream and chives or spring onions and blend well. Season to taste with pepper.

Horseradish Cream Sauce
Serves 4

This sauce is excellent served with fish, especially herring, salads.

$\frac{1}{4}$ pint/125ml soured cream
1 tablespoon grated horseradish

salt and freshly milled black pepper

Blend all the ingredients together and chill for at least 2 hours before serving.

Kren (Austrian Horseradish Sauce)
Serves 4–6

¼ pint/125ml double cream
1 tablespoon finely grated
   horseradish
1 tablespoon finely grated beetroot

2 teaspoons vinegar
pinch sugar
salt and freshly milled black pepper

Lightly whip the cream until it just holds its shape. Fold in the horseradish and beetroot, then add the vinegar and sugar and season to taste.

Basic Vanilla Ice Cream
Serves 4

2 eggs, separated
2 oz/50g sieved icing sugar

few drops vanilla essence
¼ pint/125ml double cream

Whisk the egg whites until they form stiff peaks, then beat in the sugar a teaspoonful at a time. When all the sugar has been incorporated, blend the egg yolks with the vanilla essence and beat them in. Whip the cream until it just holds its shape and fold into the egg mixture. Turn into a container and freeze for 4 hours until firm.

Variations

Coffee: Beat the egg yolks with 2 tablespoons strong sweetened black coffee, then beat into the egg whites.

Rum and Raisin: Soak 2 oz/50g of raisins in 2 tablespoons rum for 20 minutes. Fold into the mixture after the cream has been added.

Honey and Brandy: Beat the egg yolks with 2 tablespoons clear honey and 2 tablespoons brandy and beat into the egg whites.

Cassata: Fold 2 oz/50g chopped candied peel and 2 tablespoons chopped nuts into the ice cream after the cream has been folded in.

Hungarian Mocha Ice Cream
Serves 4

2 tablespoons strong black coffee
5 oz/125g plain chocolate

½ pint/250ml double cream

Put the coffee into a basin and add the chocolate, broken into small pieces. Stand the basin over a pan of hot, not boiling, water and leave until the chocolate has melted, then remove from the heat. Whip the cream until it just holds its shape, then beat in the coffee and chocolate mixture. Turn into a freezing container and freeze for 4 hours or until firm.

58

Wine Posset

Serves 4

grated rind and juice 1 large lemon
4 tablespoons white wine
2 oz/50g caster sugar
½ pint/250ml double cream

2 egg whites
To decorate:
½ lemon, thinly sliced

Place the grated lemon rind and juice, the wine, and the sugar into a bowl. Stir until the sugar has dissolved. Add the cream, then whisk the mixture until it forms soft peaks. Stiffly whisk the egg whites and fold into the mixture. Turn into 4 glasses and refrigerate for about 4 hours. Decorate with a twist of lemon before serving.

Whisky Cream

Serves 4

4 tablespoons cold water
¼ oz/7g powdered gelatine
¼ pint/125ml double cream

¼ pint/125ml single cream
1 heaped tablespoon clear honey
2 tablespoons whisky

Pour the water into a basin, sprinkle over the gelatine, and leave to soften for 5 minutes. Stand the basin over a pan of hot water and leave until the gelatine has dissolved. Whip the double and single cream together until thick. Blend the honey and whisky together and beat into the cream, then fold in the dissolved gelatine. Turn into four small pots and chill for 1 hour or until the cream has set.

CHEESE

It never ceases to amaze me that such different cheeses as Cheddar, Camembert, and Stilton are produced from cows' milk alone. Even after it has been made, all the different dishes that can be created from it make cheese one of the most versatile foods we eat. With only a little imagination one can make a wealth of cheese salads using hard cheeses, such as Cheddar, Edam, and Gruyère, or crumbled Blue cheeses, such as Stilton, Roquefort, or Danish Blue, while cream and cottage cheeses blend well with a wide variety of vegetables and fruit. In fact there are a number of desserts which are made wih cream and cottage cheese, such as the French classic *Cœurs à la Crème* and the Russian *Pashka*, as well as the more familiar cheesecake.

To Make Curd Cheese

If you want to, it is not difficult to make your own fresh curd cheese. Allow about 3 pints/1.5 litres of milk to turn sour, then pour it into a piece of muslin, hang it up and leave to drain for 12 hours. To this you can then either add seasoning and fresh herbs and a little butter or cream if you wish, or you can add some fresh cream and sugar and eat it as a dessert.

Savoury Dishes

Creamy Watercress Dip
Serves 8–10

8 oz/200g cream cheese
about 3 tablespoons milk
½ bunch watercress

1 tablespoon finely chopped onion
1 small clove garlic, crushed
salt and freshly milled black pepper

Beat the cream cheese, then gradually add the milk until the mixture is smooth and creamy. Discard about 1 inch/2.5cm of the watercress stalks and chop the remainder finely. Add to the cream cheese with the onion, garlic, and seasoning. Blend well and leave the dip for at least 2 hours or, preferably, overnight for the flavours to infuse. If necessary, add a little more milk before serving to give a good dipping consistency, i.e. soft enough to be able to dip the vegetables into the mixture without breaking them, but not so soft that it drips down everybody's clothes and onto your carpet! Serve the dip with plenty of fresh vegetables; for example, cauliflower and broccoli florets, cucumber, carrot and celery sticks, strips of red and green pepper, and radishes.

Cheese Olives
Makes 30

These are quick to prepare and make a slightly unusual appetizer to serve with drinks.

4 oz/100g walnuts
8 oz/200g cream cheese

15 stuffed olives

Finely chop the walnuts and put onto a large plate. Beat the cream cheese, then mould a heaped teaspoon round each olive to completely enclose it. Toss in the chopped walnuts, then chill for at least 1 hour. Just before serving, cut in half, using a sharp knife.

Cream Cheese with Herbs and Garlic

Serves 6

8 oz/200g cream cheese
1 tablespoon chopped chives
1 tablespoon chopped parsley
1 tablespoon chopped chervil (or
 use extra parsley)

2 teaspoons chopped tarragon
1 clove garlic, crushed
salt and freshly milled black pepper
To garnish:
2 teaspoons chopped chives

Turn the cream cheese into a basin and beat in the chives, parsley, chervil (if using), tarragon, and garlic. Season to taste with salt and pepper, then turn into a serving bowl. Cover and leave for at least 2 hours, or overnight, for the flavours to infuse. Sprinkle with the chopped chives before serving. Accompany with bread or biscuits.

Variations: Add either 1 tablespoon finely chopped celery or 1 teaspoon finely chopped onion. Alternatively, omit the herbs and use only the garlic and plenty of freshly milled black pepper.

Polish Cottage Cheese Spread

Serves 4

4 oz/100g cottage cheese
1 tablespoon single cream
1 inch/2.5cm piece cucumber

$\frac{1}{4}$ teaspoon salt
3 radishes
1 tablespoon chopped chives

Turn the cottage cheese into a basin, add the cream, and beat until the mixture is light. Peel and dice the cucumber, put into a colander and sprinkle with the salt. Leave to drain for 15 minutes. Slice the radishes very thinly and add to the cottage cheese with the cucumber and chopped chives. Season with a little extra salt, if necessary. Serve spread on bread or cream crackers, or as a dip.

Potted Cheese

Serves 4

Potted cheese is a traditional old English dish and recipes for it can be found in many old cookery books. Needless to say these recipes vary considerably, especially in the ratio between cheese and butter, but I find the proportion given below very satisfactory. The port or sherry in the recipe can be omitted if wished, and extra chopped herbs added instead. If you want to store the potted cheese for several days, do not garnish it with walnut halves as in the recipe, but cover the top with clarified butter, then put into the refrigerator

3 oz/75g unsalted butter
8 oz/200g Cheshire cheese, finely
 grated
2 tablespoons port or brown sherry

1 tablespoon chopped chives
pinch cayenne pepper
To garnish:
a few walnut halves

Cream the butter, then gradually beat in the grated cheese. Stir in the port or sherry, chives, and pepper and blend well. Spoon into 1 large or 4 small pots and chill for at least 1 hour. Garnish with walnut halves before serving.

American Tomato Cheese Mould
Serves 4

1 pint/500ml tomato juice
½ oz/15g powdered gelatine
1 teaspoon Worcestershire sauce
2 oz/50g cream cheese
4 oz/100g Cheddar cheese, finely
    grated

1 tablespoon mayonnaise
about 1 tablespoon milk (see
    method)
To garnish:
sprigs of watercress

Put 4 tablespoons of the tomato juice into a basin. Sprinkle over the gelatine and leave to soften for 5 minutes. Stand the basin over a pan of gently simmering water and leave until the gelatine has dissolved. Stir into the remainder of the tomato juice with the Worcestershire sauce and blend well. Pour half into the bottom of a rinsed mould and leave until set. Stand the remainder in a warm place so that it does not set. Beat the cream cheese, then add the Cheddar cheese, mayonnaise, and milk, and blend well. The mixture should spread easily, so if it is too thick, add a little extra milk. Spread carefully over the set jelly in the mould, then spoon the remaining tomato mixture over the top. Chill in the refrigerator for at least 2 hours or until set. To serve, dip the mould into hot water for a few seconds to loosen the jelly, then invert onto a serving plate. Garnish with sprigs of watercress.

Cauliflower Cheese Salad
Serves 4

1 small cauliflower
¼ pint/125ml mayonnaise
3 oz/75g Cheddar cheese, finely
    grated

1 teaspoon made English mustard
To garnish:
paprika

Break the cauliflower into florets. Blend the mayonnaise with the cheese and mustard in a bowl. Add the cauliflower and mix well so that the cauliflower is well coated. Cover and chill for 4 hours. Turn into a serving dish and sprinkle with the paprika before serving.

Salad Aveyronnaise
Serves 4

2 oz/50g Roquefort cheese
generous ¼ pint/150ml single cream
1 teaspoon vinegar or lemon juice
2 teaspoons chopped tarragon

2 teaspoons chopped chervil
salt and freshly milled black pepper
1 large lettuce

Mash the cheese, then stir in the cream and vinegar or lemon juice. Add the tarragon and chervil and season to taste. Wash the lettuce, tear the leaves, and dry well. Put into a polythene bag in the refrigerator and leave for at least 1 hour to crisp. Put the lettuce into a salad bowl, pour over the dressing and toss so that each lettuce leaf is coated with the cheese dressing.

◀ Potted Cheese

Greek Island Salad

Serves 4

If you find it difficult to obtain Feta cheese for this traditional Greek salad, you could substitute white Stilton.

4 oz/100g Feta cheese
4 large tomatoes, preferably
   Mediterranean-type ones
1 onion
2 oz/50g black olives, preferably
   Greek ones

2 teaspoons coriander seeds,
   crushed
1 clove garlic, crushed
1 teaspoon chopped oregano
4 tablespoons olive oil
salt and freshly milled black pepper

Cut the cheese into thin strips about 1½ inches/3.75cm long, or if white Stilton is used, crumble it. Put into a salad bowl. Slice the tomatoes and thinly slice the onion. Add to the bowl with the olives. Crush the coriander seeds and put into a screw-topped jar with all the remaining ingredients. Shake until they are all thoroughly blended. Pour over the salad just before serving and toss well.

Danish Cheese Salad

Serves 2–3

1 red pepper
1 green pepper
4 tablespoons corn oil
1 tablespoon lemon juice
pinch dry mustard

salt and freshly milled black pepper
4 oz/100g Samsoe cheese, diced
2 oz/50g Danish Blue cheese,
   crumbled
1 onion, finely chopped

Slice the peppers finely into rings, discarding the cores and seeds, and turn into a serving bowl. Put the oil, lemon juice, mustard, and seasoning into a screw-topped jar and shake until the mixture is well blended, then pour over the peppers and leave to marinate for 4 hours. Dice the Samsoe cheese and crumble the Danish Blue. Add to the peppers with the onion and toss all the ingredients together.

Cottage Cheese Grapefruit Cups

Serves 4

2 large grapefruit
few crisp lettuce leaves
¼ cucumber

12 oz/300g cottage cheese
To garnish:
few sprigs of watercress

Halve the grapefruit, cut round them with a sharp, stainless-steel knife and remove the flesh. Discard any membrane and pith. Cut the flesh into ½ inch/1.25cm pieces. Line the grapefruit skins with the lettuce leaves. Dice the cucumber and blend with the cottage cheese and grapefruit. Pile back into the grapefruit skins and garnish with the watercress before serving.

Desserts

Slimmers' Orange Dessert
Serves 4–6

juice of 1 orange
juice of ½ large lemon
1½ teaspoons powdered gelatine
12 oz/200g cottage cheese

6 tablespoons buttermilk
liquid artificial sweetener (optional)
To decorate:
1 orange, thinly sliced

Pour the orange and lemon juice into a small basin. Sprinkle over the gelatine and leave to soften for 5 minutes. Stand the basin over a pan of gently simmering water and leave until the gelatine has dissolved. Put into a blender with the cottage cheese and buttermilk and blend until smooth. Taste and adjust the sweetness with a little artificial sweetner, if required. Pour into 4–6 small glasses or dishes and chill until set. Decorate with slices of orange just before serving.

Pashka
Serves 8

Pashka is the Russian name for Easter and this famous dessert was always served on Easter Sunday. It should be made in a special mould with holes in it for the whey to run out of the cheese, but these are not easy to obtain and it can be made very successfully in a colander.

1 lb/800g fresh cream cheese
8 oz/200g unsalted butter
8 oz/200g caster sugar
4 egg yolks

few drops vanilla essence
1 lb/400g mixed chopped sultanas,
    glacé pineapple, cherries,
    angelica, and almonds

Sieve the cream cheese. Cream the butter, then beat in the sugar and gradually beat in the egg yolks until the mixture is light and fluffy. Add the cream cheese and the vanilla essence and blend well, then stir in the chopped fruit and nuts. Line a colander with muslin, put the pashka mixture in and put a plate with a heavy weight on top. Leave to drain for 12 hours in a cool place or refrigerator. Be sure to put a bowl or tray under the colander to catch the dripping whey. Turn the pashka out onto a plate before serving.

Cassata alla Siciliana (Sicilian Cream Cheese Pudding)
Serves 6

Despite its name, this is not the famous ice cream dessert, the recipe for which will be found on page 58 but a Sicilian cream cheese pudding.

12 oz/300g ricotta or other fresh
  cream cheese
6 oz/150g caster sugar

4 oz/100g plain chocolate
4 oz/100g candied peel

Sieve the cream cheese into a bowl, then beat in the sugar. Chop the chocolate fairly finely, but it should not be as fine as grated chocolate. If you prefer you could use chopped chocolate chips. Add to the cream cheese with the peel and chill for 3 hours before serving. Serve with biscuits.
Note: In Italy this dessert is sometimes made into a sort of Charlotte Russe. Line the inside of a 6 inch/15cm loose-bottomed cake tin with sponge finger biscuits and spoon the cream cheese into the middle. Chill in the refrigerator until just before serving, then remove from the tin.

Chilled Lemon Cheesecake
Serves 6–8

grated rind and juice of 2 large
  lemons
3 eggs, separated
4 oz/100g caster sugar
4 tablespoons water
½ oz/15g powdered gelatine
¼ pint/125ml single cream

12 oz/300g cottage cheese, sieved
¼ pint/125ml double cream, lightly
  whipped
For the crust:
4 oz/100g digestive biscuits
2 tablespoons demerara sugar
2 oz/50g butter, melted

Put the lemon rind and juice into a bowl with the egg yolks and caster sugar. Stand the bowl over a pan of simmering water and whisk until thick and foamy. Remove the bowl from the heat and whisk until cool. Put the water into a basin, sprinkle over the gelatine and leave to stand for 5 minutes. Put the basin over a pan of hot water and leave until the gelatine has dissolved. Blend the single cream into the cottage cheese, then carefully blend in the egg-yolk mixture and gelatine. Put on one side until slightly thickened, but not set. Whisk the egg whites until they are stiff, then fold first the cream and then the egg whites into the cheese mixture. Turn into a lightly buttered 8 inch/20cm loose-bottomed cake tin and chill. Mix together the crushed biscuits, demerara sugar, and melted butter and sprinkle this mixture over the set cheesecake. Press down lightly. To serve, turn the cheesecake out of the tin on to a serving plate, so that the crust is underneath. Decorate with fresh fruit if liked.

Cream Cheese with Wine
Serves 4–6

1 lb/400g fresh cream cheese
4 oz/100g caster sugar (see method)

5 tablespoons white wine
juice of 1 lemon

Sieve the cheese into a bowl, then beat in the sugar and gradually beat in the wine and lemon juice. Taste the mixture and add a little more sugar if necessary; the amount of sugar required will depend on the type of wine used. Either turn into a serving bowl or into individual glasses or dishes. Chill for at least 2 hours and serve with fresh fruit or biscuits.

Crème Saint Valentin
Serves 6

8 oz/200g cream cheese
3 eggs, separated

2 oz/50g caster sugar
2 teaspoons instant coffee

Beat together the cheese, egg yolks, sugar, and coffee. Leave to stand for 10 minutes for the coffee to dissolve, then beat again. Whisk the egg whites until they stand in soft peaks, then fold into the cheese mixture. Turn into small individual dishes and chill.

Cœurs à la crème
Serves 6

This dessert gets its name because it is traditionally made in small, heart-shaped china or tin moulds. These can be bought from kitchen-equipment stores, but it can be made very satisfactorily in a small sieve or colander, although it will not be quite as attractive.

8 oz/200g cottage cheese
½ pint/250ml double cream

2–3 tablespoons caster sugar

Sieve the cottage cheese into a basin. Stir in the cream and sugar and mix well. Line either small moulds or a sieve or colander with muslin and press in the cheese mixture. Leave overnight in the refrigerator to drain. Be sure to place the mould(s) on a tray to catch the dripping whey. Unmould the cheese, arrange on a serving dish and surround with fresh fruit; strawberries, raspberries, peaches, black-currants, etc. Serve with extra sugar and fresh cream.

VEGETABLES & SALADS

ALMOST ALL vegetables can be eaten raw and, nutritionally, are more valuable eaten this way as, even with careful cooking, many of the vitamins and minerals which are found in them are lost. Vegetable dishes and salads of different kinds can form complete meals in themselves; they can be used as a side dish to serve with fish, meat, eggs or cheese; and they make excellent hors d'œuvres.

Summer is usually thought of as the time for eating salads, but it is in the winter that one needs a larger supply of Vitamin C to help build up one's resistance to colds and 'flu. Although lettuce, cucumber, and tomatoes can now be bought all the year round, the quality is generally not as good during the winter and they are usually very expensive. Excellent crisp salads can be made of winter vegetables such as celeriac, cabbage, carrots, and chicory and you will find several recipes for these vegetables in this chapter.

All vegetables to be eaten raw should first be washed in plenty of cold water to remove any dirt, grit, and insects. Salad vegetables such as lettuce, endive, and watercress crisp up well if you wash them a few hours before you want to use them, shake off the excess water, then put them into a polythene bag in the refrigerator. If possible vegetables which are going to be shredded or grated, such as cabbage and carrots, should only be prepared shortly before serving as some of the vitamins and minerals are lost after shredding or grating.

Avocado Pears

Technically an avocado pear is a fruit rather than a vegetable and there are recipes for serving them as a sweet dish in the fruit chapter, but they are more commonly served as a savoury food. Unlike most other fruit and vegetables, other than peas and beans, avocado pears have a high protein content, and their fat content is only slightly less than that of the olive.

The simplest way to serve an avocado pear is just to cut it carefully in half,

70

remove the stone and fill the centre, where the stone was removed, with French dressing. Although it is now cultivated throughout the world, the fruit originated in tropical America and it is from there that some of the most delicious recipes for using it come.

Guacamole
Serves 4

This is a famous Mexican speciality and in this, as in some of the other recipes below, you can use slightly over-ripe pears which can often be bought slightly cheaper.

1 large avocado pear	2 large tomatoes
1 tablespoon lemon juice	salt
1 small onion, peeled and grated	few drops Tabasco sauce
1 clove garlic, crushed	2 tablespoons olive oil

Peel the pear, remove the stone, and mash the flesh. Add the lemon juice, onion, and garlic. Peel the tomatoes, cut them into quarters and remove the pips. Chop the flesh and add to the avocado mixture with the salt, Tabasco, and oil. Mix well, then taste and adjust the seasoning. Serve lightly chilled with lettuce and a wedge of lemon, if liked.

Avocado and Celery Appetizer
Serves 4

2 avocado pears	few drops Tabasco sauce
1 tablespoon lemon juice	salt and freshly milled black pepper
4 sticks celery, chopped	To garnish:
4 heaped tablespoons mayonnaise	few celery leaves

Peel the avocado pears, cut them in half, and remove the stones. Cut the flesh into neat pieces. Put into a basin, then pour over the lemon juice and toss lightly. Add the celery, mayonnaise, Tabasco, and seasoning and mix well. Turn into four individual serving bowls and garnish each one with a few celery leaves.

Grapefruit and Avocado Vinaigrette
Serves 4

1 large grapefruit	1 tablespoon lemon juice
1 large avocado pear	pinch sugar
3 tablespoons olive oil	salt and freshly milled black pepper

Using a very sharp knife, peel off all the skin and pith of the grapefruit. Hold the grapefruit over a basin and cut out the segments of fruit, discarding the membrane and any pips. Peel the avocado pear, cut in half, and remove the stone. Slice the flesh thinly. Arrange the grapefruit segments and avocado slices in four individual dishes or glasses. Mix the remaining ingredients with the grapefruit juice in the basin and spoon over the fruit immediately to preserve the colour.

71

Walnut and Avocado Salad
Serves 4

This salad can be served as a starter or, if served with another salad, makes an excellent light lunch or supper as the mixture of avocado pears and nuts is very high in both protein and fat.

2 avocado pears
2 tablespoons lemon juice
2 dessert apples
2 oz/50g chopped walnuts
3 tablespoons olive oil
2 cloves garlic, crushed

pinch dry mustard
salt and freshly milled black pepper
To garnish:
few lettuce leaves
¼ cucumber, thinly sliced

Cut the avocado pears in half, remove the stones, and carefully scoop out the flesh, taking care not to spoil the skin of the pear. Mash the flesh with the lemon juice. Peel and core the apples and chop finely. Add to the avocado purée with the walnuts, oil, garlic, mustard, and seasoning. Taste and adjust the seasoning. Pile the mixture back into the avocado shells and arrange on individual plates. Garnish with lettuce and cucumber.

Broad Beans

Broad Bean Salad with Basil
Serves 4

1 lb/400g fresh shelled, young
   broad beans
1 small onion
6 black olives

1 tablespoon chopped basil
5 tablespoons olive oil
2 tablespoons wine vinegar
salt and freshly milled black pepper

Put the beans into a serving bowl. Chop the onion finely and stone the olives. Add to the beans with the basil. Blend the oil, vinegar, and seasoning in a screw-topped jar, then pour over the beans. Toss the ingredients to mix them and leave to marinate in a cool place for 4 hours before serving.

72

Cabbage

The ideal cabbage for salads is the hard white 'Dutch' cabbage, but other types of cabbage can be used. It is, however, important that the cabbage is very crisp and firm and, preferably, it should not have thick stalks and veins in the leaves as these are likely to be tough. Always discard any tough outer leaves before the cabbage is shredded and, if it appears to have slugs or any other insects, it should first be soaked in a little salt water. Rinse afterwards in plenty of fresh cold water and dry well. It is obviously best to use the cabbage as fresh as possible, but if you buy a large cabbage and find you only want to use half of it, the remainder will keep for several days in the refrigerator if covered with self-clinging wrap.

Basic Coleslaw

1 lb/400g white cabbage
1 small onion
4 oz/100g carrots

¼ pint/125ml mayonnaise
salt and freshly milled black pepper

Shred the cabbage finely: this can be done by using a sharp knife, a grater, or a hand-operated or mechanical shredder – all that is important is that the cabbage is shredded finely and evenly, without any coarse stalks. Chop the onion very finely and shred or grate the carrots. Put the vegetables into a bowl, and stir in the mayonnaise. Mix well and season to taste.

Variations

Pineapple Slaw Add 2 slices finely chopped pineapple and a tablespoon of chopped nuts, if wished.

Apple and Raisin Slaw Add 1 chopped dessert apple, tossed in a very little lemon juice to preserve the colour, and 2 tablespoons seedless raisins.

Raisin and Nut Slaw Add 2 tablespoons seedless raisins and 2 tablespoons chopped nuts – walnuts, hazelnuts, almonds, or a mixture.

Cheese Slaw Add 4 oz/100g cheese, cut into thin matchsticks. Use Cheddar, Edam, Gouda, or a Swiss cheese.

Pepper Slaw Add a small, finely shredded green and red pepper.

Soured Cream Slaw Replace half or all the mayonnaise with soured cream and season well.

Slimmer's Slaw Replace the mayonnaise with natural yogurt and season well.

Royal Slaw
Serves 4

1 lb/400g red cabbage	4 tablespoons olive or corn oil
2–3 sticks celery	2 tablespoons vinegar
1 dessert apple	$\frac{1}{2}$ teaspoon French mustard
1 large banana	salt and freshly milled black pepper

Thinly shred the cabbage, discarding any tough outer leaves and the centre core, and put into a mixing bowl. Finely chop the celery, core and finely chop the apple, thinly slice the banana and add them to the cabbage. Put all the remaining ingredients into a screw-topped jar and shake until well blended. Pour over the cabbage and fruit, toss well and leave for at least 30 minutes before serving.

Jamaican Sour Sweet Salad
Serves 4

2 oranges	salt and freshly milled black pepper
2 tablespoons lime juice	To garnish:
1 dessert apple	3 tomatoes, sliced
1 lb/400g white cabbage	$\frac{1}{4}$ cucumber, sliced

Peel the oranges, discarding all the white pith. Holding the fruit over a bowl so that you catch any juice which comes out, cut the fruit into segments. Squeeze out all the juice from the pith. Put the segments into the bowl with the orange juice and add the lime juice. Grate the apple and shred the cabbage finely, discarding any withered leaves and the centre core. Add to the orange and lime juice in the bowl, season with salt and pepper and toss well together. Turn into a serving bowl and garnish with the tomatoes and cucumber.

To Make Sauerkraut

As cabbage does not freeze well, sauerkraut is an excellent method of preserving it if you find you have grown too many, or they are particularly cheap in the shops.

6 firm cabbages	2 tablespoons black peppercorns
1 lb/400g coarse kitchen salt	2 tablespoons juniper berries

Remove all the outer leaves from the cabbages. Cut the cabbages into quarters, remove the centre stalks, then shred finely. Press a layer of shredded cabbage into a large crock and sprinkle with salt and a few peppercorns and juniper berries. Continue these layers until all the ingredients have been used, pressing the cabbage down well. Cover with several layers of muslin, then put a plate on top and place a heavy weight on this. Store in a larder or cool place. After a few days fermentation will start and the plate will eventually sink under the salt water that has formed. Remove some of the brine, but leave enough to cover the plate. The sauerkraut will be ready for eating after one month. When you remove some sauerkraut from the crock, wash the plate and the muslin before replacing them and pour a little fresh water over to cover. Always wash the sauerkraut in fresh water before using, either for serving in salads or for cooking.

Sauerkraut Salad

Serves 4

1 lb/400g sauerkraut
1 tablespoon wine vinegar
2 tablespoons oil

1 small onion, finely chopped
½ teaspoon fennel seeds
freshly milled black pepper

Put the sauerkraut into a bowl, cover with cold water and leave to soak for 10 minutes. Drain, then wring dry in a tea towel. Put into a bowl and add the vinegar, oil, onion, fennel, and pepper and mix well. Leave for at least 10 minutes for the flavours to infuse before serving.

Sauerkraut with Soured Cream

Serves 4–6

1 lb/400g sauerkraut
2 tablespoons white wine
¼ pint/125ml soured cream

1 small onion, finely chopped
freshly milled black pepper

Put the sauerkraut into a bowl, cover with cold water for 10 minutes, then drain. Put into a clean tea towel and wring dry. Turn the sauerkraut into a bowl and stir in the white wine, cream, and onion and season with plenty of freshly milled black pepper. Leave for at least 10 minutes for the flavours to infuse before serving.

Carrots

Although fresh, young carrots will taste delicious, if you want to grate them it is generally better to have slightly larger, older carrots. Otherwise, especially if you are grating by hand, you will find you have a great deal of wastage (as well as the possibility of a few slightly sore fingers!). Wash the carrots, then scrape or peel them and grate coarsely.

Carrot and Cheese Salad

Serves 4

4 oz/100g curd or cream cheese
2 tablespoons lemon juice
1 clove garlic, crushed
2 tablespoons seedless raisins

salt and freshly milled black pepper
8 oz/200g carrots
To garnish:
sprigs of watercress

Beat the cheese, and beat in the lemon juice, garlic, raisins, and seasoning. Peel and grate the carrots, then stir into the cheese mixture. Pile on to a serving dish and garnish with sprigs of watercress.

Celeriac and Celery

Celeriac Salad

Serves 4–6

This makes a very good and comparatively inexpensive winter salad. It can either be served with another salad and cold meats for a main dish or is excellent served as a starter with Parma ham and/or salami. If you prefer, you can soften the celeriac by blanching it in boiling water for a minute.

1 medium-sized celeriac, about 1$\frac{1}{2}$
    lb/600g in weight
$\frac{1}{2}$ pint/250ml mayonnaise
1 tablespoon chopped parsley

1 dill cucumber, finely chopped
salt and freshly milled black pepper
To garnish:
paprika

Peel the celeriac and cut into matchstick pieces. Put into a bowl and add the mayonnaise, parsley, dill cucumber, and seasoning. Mix well and either turn into a salad bowl or arrange with ham or salami on individual plates and sprinkle with paprika to garnish.

76

Celery Rémoulade

Serves 4

1 small head celery
generous ¼ pint/150ml Rémoulade sauce (page 48)

Take off the outside sticks of the celery; these can be used for soups or flavouring casseroles, etc. Wash the remainder, dry well, and cut diagonally into thin strips. Reserve the very centre leaves for garnish. If you like, the celery strips can be blanched in boiling salted water for 1 minute, then drained and quickly rinsed in cold water and dried well. Blend the celery with the Rémoulade sauce, turn into a serving bowl, and garnish with the reserved celery leaves.

Californian Stuffed Celery

Serves 6

1 large head celery
4 oz/100g tenderized prunes
4 oz/100g cream cheese

2 oz/50g Cheddar cheese, grated
1 tablespoon mayonnaise
salt and freshly milled black pepper

Carefully pull apart the head of celery. Discard any very tough outer stalks and trim the remainder neatly. Finely chop the very centre stalks of the celery. Stone the prunes and chop them finely. Beat the cream cheese, then beat in the Cheddar cheese and mayonnaise. Stir in the prunes and finely chopped celery heart and season to taste with salt and pepper. Press some of this mixture into each celery stalk then reassemble the head. Tie into place with string, if necessary, then chill in the refrigerator for 3 hours. To serve the celery, use a very sharp knife and cut across into circles.

Chicory

Belgian Chicory Salad

Serves 4

4 medium-sized chicory spears
2 tablespoons olive oil
1 tablespoon lemon juice

½ teaspoon sugar
salt and freshly milled black pepper
2 tablespoons chopped parsley

Finely slice the chicory and put into a serving dish. Put the oil, lemon juice, sugar, and seasoning into a screw-topped jar and shake until well blended. Pour over the chicory and sprinkle with the chopped parsley.

Chicory Hors d'Oeuvre

Serves 4–6

1 lb/400g chicory spears
juice 1 large lemon
1 egg yolk
salt and freshly milled black pepper

¼ pint/125ml oil
1 small red pepper
1 small green pepper

Cut the base off each head of chicory. Separate the leaves, wash well, and dry thoroughly. Put into a bowl, pour over the lemon juice, toss lightly and leave for 15 minutes. Beat the egg yolk with a little seasoning. Gradually beat in the oil a drop at a time, then add the lemon juice, drained from the chicory. Taste and adjust the seasoning, then add a little warm water, if necessary, to give a stiff pouring consistency. Finely chop the peppers, discarding the cores and seeds. Divide the chicory among 4–6 small bowls or wide-necked glasses. Just before serving, spoon over the dressing and sprinkle with the chopped peppers.

Cucumber

The delicate flavour of cucumber has made it an essential ingredient of many salads, but I feel it is at its best served on its own, without being blended with other vegetables. Because of its high water content, it is always advisable to salt the cucumber about 30 minutes before mixing with a dressing. This helps draw out the excess liquid so that the salad does not become watery. For most salads, I prefer the cucumber to be peeled, but this is obviously a matter of personal choice.

Cucumber Salad

Serves 4

1 cucumber
2 teaspoons salt
2 tablespoons olive or corn oil
1 teaspoon vinegar

pinch sugar
1 tablespoon chopped chives
1 tablespoon chopped parsley

Peel the cucumber and cut into very thin slices; the best way to do this is with a mandoline if you have one, or use the slicing part of a grater. Put the cucumber into a colander and sprinkle it with the salt. Press it down with a plate and leave to drain

78

for about 30 minutes. Dry the cucumber well with a clean tea towel or kitchen paper. Put into a salad bowl, add the remaining ingredients and toss lightly.
Note: For a Scandinavian cucumber salad, omit the chives and sprinkle the salad with chopped fresh dill, or with dill seeds, before serving.

Turkish Cucumber Salad
Serves 4

½ large cucumber
1 teaspoon salt
½ pint/250ml natural yogurt

1 clove garlic, crushed
1 tablespoon chopped mint

Peel the cucumber and slice thinly (see above). Put into a colander, sprinkle with salt, and put a plate on top. Leave to drain for 30 minutes, then dry well. Turn the yogurt into a bowl, add the garlic and mint, then stir in the cucumber and mix well. Turn into a serving dish and chill for 1 hour before serving.

Cucumber Salad with Cream
Serves 4

1 large cucumber
1 teaspoon sea salt
1 teaspoon sugar
1 teaspoon vinegar, preferably
  tarragon vinegar

4 tablespoons single cream
2 tablespoons olive oil
freshly milled black pepper
1 tablespoon chopped chives

Peel the cucumber and cut into very thin slices. Put into a colander, sprinkle over the salt, and leave to drain for 30 minutes. Blend the sugar and vinegar together, then add the cream, oil, pepper, a little salt, and the chives. Turn the cucumber into a shallow dish and pour over the dressing. Do not leave the salad standing for too long before serving after the dressing has been added.

Dandelions

Dandelions for salads must be young and tender, or they will be stringy and bitter. If they are growing in your garden it is a good idea to blanch them by covering them with pots a few days before you want to use them as this helps to reduce bitterness.

French Dandelion Salad
Serves 3–4

about 4 oz/100g fresh dandelion
  leaves
1 shallot, finely chopped
1 clove garlic, crushed

1 tablespoon chopped chives
salt and freshly milled black pepper
1 tablespoon wine vinegar
3 tablespoons olive oil

Wash the dandelion leaves thoroughly and discard any tough ones. Dry well and place in a salad bowl. Put all the remaining ingredients into a screw-topped jar and shake until well blended. Pour over the salad and toss lightly.

Fennel

Florence fennel makes a useful addition to green salads. Discard the tough outer sheaths and slice the root finely.

Fennel Salad
Serves 4

2 Florence fennel roots
5 tablespoons olive oil
2 tablespoons lemon juice

pinch dry mustard
salt and freshly milled black pepper
1 tablespoon chopped chives
  (optional)

Wash the fennel and discard any very tough outer parts. Cut into thin strips and place in a serving dish. Put the oil, lemon juice, mustard, and seasoning into a screw-topped jar and shake until well blended. Pour over the fennel, cover and chill for 2–3 hours. Sprinkle with the chopped chives, if liked, just before serving.

Leeks

Leek and Tomato Salad
Serves 6

1 small lettuce
4 tender young leeks
4 tomatoes
1 teaspoon chopped basil
1 teaspoon chopped chervil

2 tablespoons oil
1 tablespoon lemon juice
salt and freshly milled black pepper
pinch dry mustard
pinch sugar

Wash the lettuce, dry well, and put into a polythene bag. Put into the refrigerator and leave to crisp for 1 hour. Wash the leeks thoroughly to remove the dirt and grit. Dry, then slice crosswise very finely into rings. Cut the tomatoes into quarters. Arrange the lettuce leaves round the outside of a salad bowl. Pile the leeks and tomatoes into the centre and sprinkle with the chopped herbs. Put all the remaining ingredients into a screw-topped jar. Shake until blended, pour over the salad just before serving and toss well.

Lettuce

Lettuce Hearts with Cream Dressing
Serves 4

2 lettuce hearts
$\frac{1}{4}$ pint/125ml double cream
2 tablespoons wine vinegar
6 tablespoons olive oil
$\frac{1}{2}$ teaspoon paprika

salt and freshly milled black pepper
To garnish:
2 tablespoons chopped parsley
2 tomatoes, quartered

Wash and trim the lettuces, cut into quarters, and place in a polythene bag in the refrigerator for at least an hour to crisp. Lightly whip the cream, then beat in the vinegar and gradually beat in the oil until you have a thick creamy mixture. Add the paprika and seasoning. Arrange the lettuce quarters on a plate and spoon over the dressing. Sprinkle with the chopped parsley and garnish with the quarters of tomato.

Mushrooms

The best mushrooms to use are the small, button ones, but open flat ones can also be used. It is not necessary to peel them, simply wash in cold water and dry well, then slice or leave whole according to the recipe.

Creamy Mushroom Cocktail
Serves 4

This is a delicious, quickly prepared, vegetarian starter.

1 large tomato
3 tablespoons whipped double
  cream
4 tablespoons mayonnaise
2 teaspoons Worcestershire sauce
1 teaspoon lemon juice

1 tablespoon chopped parsley
8 oz/200g button mushrooms
salt and freshly milled black pepper
To garnish:
parsley sprigs or paprika

Peel the tomato and chop finely, discarding the seeds. Fold the cream into the mayonnaise, then stir in the tomato, Worcestershire sauce, lemon juice, and parsley. Slice the mushrooms, then stir them into the sauce and season to taste. Spoon the mixture into four individual glasses and garnish with sprigs of parsley or paprika.
Variation: Use $\frac{1}{4}$ pint/125ml soured cream in place of the whipped cream and mayonnaise.

Mushroom and Pepper Salad
Serves 4

8 anchovy fillets
1 red pepper
1 green pepper
8 oz/200g button mushrooms
6 tablespoons olive oil

2 tablespoons wine vinegar
good pinch dry mustard
pinch sugar
salt and freshly milled black pepper

Soak the anchovies for 2 hours in cold water, if very salt, or rinse under the cold tap. Cut the peppers into strips, discarding the cores and seeds, and slice the mushrooms. Put the vegetables into a bowl. Put the oil, vinegar, mustard, sugar, and seasoning into a screw-topped jar and shake well. Pour over the peppers and mushrooms and mix well. Turn into a serving dish. Cut the anchovies into thin strips and use to garnish the salad.

Mushroom Salad with Soy Sauce
Serves 6

1 lb/400g mushrooms
salt and freshly milled black pepper

2 teaspoons Worcestershire sauce
1 tablespoon soy sauce

Wipe the mushrooms and trim the bases of the stalks. Leave them whole if they are small or cut into halves or quarters if large. Put into a serving bowl and season with salt and pepper. Sprinkle over the Worcestershire and soy sauce and blend well, then chill for at least 2 hours before serving, turning the mushrooms from time to time.

83

Mushrooms with Dijon Mustard
Serves 4–6

1 lb/400g button mushrooms
juice of 2 lemons
¼ pint/125ml olive oil
½ teaspoon black peppercorns

2 bay leaves
1 tablespoon Dijon mustard
salt
2 tablespoons chopped parsley

Wipe the mushrooms and trim off the stalk ends. Cut into halves or quarters and place in a shallow dish. Blend the lemon juice with the olive oil, peppercorns, bay leaves (torn into two or three pieces), mustard, and salt. Pour over the mushrooms, cover and leave to marinate overnight, turning the mushrooms in the marinade from time to time. Remove the bay leaves, turn into a serving dish, and sprinkle with the parsley before serving.

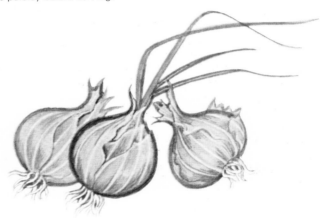

Onions

Onion Salad
Serves 4

3–4 large Spanish onions
4 tablespoons salt
1 teaspoon tarragon or other vinegar
2 tablespoons lemon juice

2 teaspoons cold water
salt and freshly milled black pepper
3 tablespoons olive oil
1 tablespoon chopped parsley

Peel the onions and cut in half lengthwise. Slice each half very thinly. Place the sliced onions in a sieve and sprinkle with the salt. Press the onions and salt together until all the salt has dissolved, then rinse the onions thoroughly under cold running water and drain well. Mix together with the vinegar, lemon juice, and water in a salad bowl and season with salt and pepper. Whisk in the olive oil gradually. Add the onion slices and parsley and mix thoroughly. Leave to stand for a few minutes before serving.

84

Peppers

Always discard the core and seeds of peppers before using. The sweet red and yellow peppers do not need blanching, but you may prefer to blanch green peppers to remove any bitterness. Simply drop the whole or sliced peppers into boiling water for 1 minute, then drain and rinse quickly in cold water.

Stuffed Pepper Salad
Serves 4

1 red pepper
1 green pepper
4 oz/100g cottage cheese
4 oz/100g cream cheese
½ small onion, finely chopped
1 tablespoon chopped chives

1 tablespoon chopped parsley
few drops Tabasco (optional)
salt and freshly milled black pepper
To garnish:
sprigs of watercress

Cut the tops off the peppers, scoop out and discard the seeds. Beat the cottage cheese with the cream cheese, onion, chives, parsley, Tabasco, if using, and seasoning. Spoon this mixture back into the peppers and press down firmly. Chill for 1 hour. To serve, slice the peppers into rings, using a sharp knife, and arrange on a serving plate. Garnish with watercress.
Variation: Add 4 chopped anchovy fillets to the cream-cheese mixture.

Green Peppers with Yogurt Dressing
Serves 4

1 medium-sized cucumber
1 teaspoon sea salt
4 green peppers
3 spring onions, finely chopped

1 tablespoon chopped tarragon
1 tablespoon chopped dill
½ pint/250ml natural yogurt
freshly milled black pepper

Peel the cucumber, cut into thin slices, and place in a colander. Sprinkle with the salt and leave for 30 minutes for the excess liquid to drain off. Discard the cores and seeds of the peppers and cut into very fine strips. Put into a bowl with the cucumber, onions, and herbs. Stir in the yogurt and blend well. Season with black pepper and a little more salt if necessary. Turn into a serving dish, cover and chill for 1 hour before serving.

Radishes

Panamanian Radish Salad
Serves 4

For this recipe you can use the ordinary red radishes or, if you grow or can buy them, the white radishes or mooli which you will find quicker to prepare.

3 bunches red radishes or
 12 oz/300g white radishes or
 mooli
1 small onion
1 large tomato

1 teaspoon chopped mint
2 tablespoons olive oil
2 tablespoons lemon juice
salt and freshly milled black pepper

Wash the radishes and slice them thinly. Chop the onion finely, and peel and finely chop the tomato. Arrange the vegetables attractively in a serving dish. Put all the remaining ingredients into a screw-topped jar and shake well. Pour over the radishes and chill lightly for 1 hour before serving.

Spinach

Spinach is an excellent salad ingredient as when raw it has enormous bulk which is lost when it is cooked. Choose tender, young leaves and wash thoroughly to

86

remove all the dirt, grit, and sand. You must make sure that the leaves are fresh and crisp and if they look a little limp they should be soaked in cold water for $\frac{1}{2}$ hour, then put into a polythene bag in the refrigerator for 1 hour.

Spinach Slaw
Serves 4–6

3 tablespoons seedless raisins
4 tablespoons lemon juice
8 oz/200g young spinach leaves
8 oz/200g white cabbage

1 dessert apple
3 tablespoons corn oil
salt and freshly milled black pepper
good pinch sugar

Put the raisins into a basin, pour over 2 tablespoons of the lemon juice and leave for 1 hour until they are plump. Wash the spinach thoroughly to remove all the grit and sand. Dry well. Shred the spinach and cabbage finely, discarding any outside leaves from the cabbage and the tough centre stalk. Peel the apple, if wished, then core and dice it. Put the spinach, cabbage, raisins, and apple into a salad bowl. Put the remaining ingredients into a screw-topped jar and shake until blended. Pour over the salad and toss well.

Spinach and Mushroom Salad
Serves 4–6

12 oz/300g young spinach leaves
8 oz/200g button mushrooms
1 small onion, finely chopped
1 tablespoon chopped parsley
6 tablespoons olive oil

1 tablespoon vinegar
1 tablespoon lemon juice
1 clove garlic, crushed
salt and freshly milled black pepper

Wash the spinach thoroughly to remove all the grit and sand. Dry well, then tear into a salad bowl. Wash or wipe the mushrooms and cut into thin slices. Add to the salad bowl with the onion. Put all the remaining ingredients into a screw-topped jar. Shake until well blended, then just before serving pour over the salad and toss.

Spinach Salad with Yogurt
Serves 4–6

8 oz/200g young spinach leaves
$\frac{1}{2}$ cucumber
$\frac{1}{4}$ pint/125ml natural yogurt
4 tablespoons olive oil

juice of 1 lemon
1 teaspoon French mustard
salt and freshly milled black pepper

Wash the spinach well to remove all the dirt, grit, and sand. Drain and dry thoroughly then tear or chop roughly. Dice the cucumber, but do not peel it. Turn the yogurt into a bowl and gradually beat in the oil and lemon juice. Add the mustard and season to taste. Add the spinach and cucumber and toss the mixture well together, then turn into a serving dish. Cover and chill for 1 hour before serving.

Tomatoes

The tomato is one of the most versatile vegetables (technically it is a fruit), being used in all sorts of salads, soups, casseroles, and sauces. Although one can now buy tomatoes all the year round, the flavour of the imported winter ones cannot compare with the taste of freshly picked summer ones, so when they are at their best and cheapest I try to make the maximum use of them. For some recipes it is best to peel the tomatoes before using, and this can be done either by covering with boiling water for a minute, then quickly draining and peeling, or by holding the tomato on a fork over a gas flame until the skin splits.

Tomato Salad with Basil
Serves 4

1 clove garlic
1½ lb/600g large tomatoes
3 tablespoons olive oil
1 tablespoon wine vinegar

salt and freshly milled black pepper
1 tablespoon finely chopped onion
1 tablespoon chopped basil

Peel the clove of garlic, cut it in half and rub all round the inside of the salad bowl to give just a faint hint of garlic. Peel the tomatoes, if wished, or leave unpeeled and cut into slices. Blend the oil with the vinegar and seasoning. Pour over the tomatoes and sprinkle with the onion and basil just before serving.

Tomatoes and Black Olives
Serves 4

1 lb/400g tomatoes
salt and freshly milled black pepper
1 clove garlic, crushed

4 tablespoons mayonnaise
2 oz/50g black olives

88

Peel the tomatoes, cut them into slices and place on a serving dish. Season with salt and pepper, cover and chill for 1 hour. Blend the garlic into the mayonnaise and spread over the tomatoes. Stone the olives, then chop them coarsely and scatter over the top of the tomatoes.

Tomatoes with Horseradish Cream
Serves 4

6 large tomatoes
few lettuce leaves
¼ pint/125ml double cream
4 tablespoons mayonnaise

1 tablespoon grated horseradish
salt and freshly milled black pepper
2 tablespoons chopped chives

Peel the tomatoes and cut them into thick slices. Arrange on four small plates with a few lettuce leaves, cover and chill until ready to serve. Lightly whip the cream, then fold in the mayonnaise, horseradish, and seasoning. Chill. Just before serving, spread the sauce over the tomatoes and sprinkle with the chopped chives.

Cheesy Stuffed Tomatoes
Serves 4

4 medium-sized tomatoes
2 oz/50g butter
2 oz/50g Gouda cheese, finely
    grated
salt and freshly milled black pepper

pinch cayenne pepper
To garnish:
paprika
few crisp lettuce leaves

Slice the tops off the tomatoes and scoop out the seeds with a teaspoon. Turn the tomatoes upside-down and leave to drain for 30 minutes. Cream the butter, then beat in the cheese and seasoning. Either spoon the cheese mixture into each tomato, or put into a piping bag with a large rose pipe and pipe into the tomato cases. Sprinkle a little paprika over the cheese mixture and arrange the tomatoes on a bed of crisp lettuce.

Cottage Cheese Stuffed Tomatoes
Serves 4

4 large tomatoes
salt and freshly milled black pepper
8 oz/200g cottage cheese

4 spring onions, chopped
1 stick celery, finely chopped
½ teaspoon made English mustard

Slice the tops off the tomatoes and scoop out the seeds with a teaspoon. Turn the tomatoes upside-down and leave to drain for 30 minutes. Season inside the tomatoes lightly with salt and pepper. Roughly chop the tomato centres and blend with the cottage cheese, spring onions, celery, mustard, and seasoning. Pile the cottage-cheese mixture back into the tomato cases and top with the lids.

Watercress

Chinese Watercress Salad
Serves 4

1 bunch watercress
1 small bunch radishes
3 sticks celery
4 tablespoons olive or soya oil

$\frac{1}{2}$ teaspoon sugar
1 tablespoon lemon juice
2 teaspoons soy sauce
salt and freshly milled black pepper

Wash the watercress, trim off the stalks, dry well, and place in a polythene bag in the refrigerator for at least 1 hour to crisp. Trim and slice the radishes and chop the celery. Put the olive or soya oil into a screw-topped jar with the sugar, lemon juice, soy sauce, and seasoning. Shake well until blended. Just before serving, place the watercress in a salad bowl with the radishes and celery, pour over the dressing and toss the salad.

MIXED SALADS

Creole Achards
Serves 6

For this hors d'œuvre you can use any mixture of raw vegetables you like, i.e. French beans, carrots, onions, cauliflower, cabbage, peas, red and green peppers, young turnips, etc.

1½ tablespoons salt
2 pints/1 litre water
1½ lb/600g mixed raw vegetables
  (see above)
1 medium-sized onion, finely
  chopped

a good pinch of saffron powder
¼ teaspoon freshly milled black
  pepper
¼–½ teaspoon chilli pepper
good pinch ground cumin
¼ pint/125ml olive oil

Dissolve the salt in the water. Prepare the vegetables according to kind, i.e. string and chop the beans, peel and dice the carrots, break the cauliflower into florets, shred the cabbage. Put each vegetable into a separate basin and cover with the brine. Leave to soak for 24 hours, then drain and dry and place in mounds in a shallow dish. Put the onion, saffron, pepper, chilli pepper, cumin, and a good pinch of salt into a saucepan with the oil. Bring to the boil, then pour over the vegetables. Cover the dish and leave in a cool place or refrigerator for 24–48 hours. Baste the vegetables with the marinade from time to time.

Ironmongers' Salad
Serves 4

4 large tomatoes
2 green peppers
1 large onion
salt
1 teaspoon finely chopped parsley
½ teaspoon finely chopped mint

2 tablespoons lemon juice
1 teaspoon vinegar
2 tablespoons olive oil
freshly milled black pepper
8–10 black olives

Peel the tomatoes. Cut them in quarters and scoop out the seeds. Place the seeds in a sieve over a bowl and press them until all the juice has run into the bowl. Discard the seeds, but reserve the juice. Cut the peppers in half, discard the cores and seeds and slice finely. Peel the onion and cut into very fine rings. Place the onion slices in a sieve and sprinkle with salt. Press the onion and salt together until the salt has dissolved and the juice runs out from the onion. Rinse the onion well under cold water then drain and dry thoroughly. Blend the reserved tomato juice with the parsley, mint, lemon juice, vinegar, oil and seasoning. Add the quartered tomatoes, peppers, onion and olives and mix well. Leave the salad for 30 minutes before serving for the flavours to infuse.

Italian Mixed Salad
Serves 4

2 peppers, preferably yellow ones,
  but red or green can be used
2 large tomatoes
4 radishes

1 large stick celery
2 tablespoons olive oil
salt and freshly milled black pepper

Slice the peppers into rings, discarding the cores and seeds. Peel and slice the tomatoes, thinly slice the radishes and chop the celery. Put all the vegetables into a shallow dish, pour over the oil and season with salt and pepper.

Smith Salad
Serves 4

2 oz/50g anchovy fillets
1 small cauliflower
1 round lettuce heart
1 small cos lettuce
2 heads chicory
1 small bunch watercress

4 oz/100g sliced salami
4 oz/100g Gruyère cheese
5 tablespoons olive oil
2 tablespoons vinegar
½ teaspoon French mustard
salt and freshly milled black pepper

Soak the anchovy fillets in cold water for 2 hours, if they are very salt. If not, rinse them under a cold tap to remove the excess salt, then drain and slice. Break the cauliflower into florets. Wash the lettuces, dry well, then shred them. Slice the chicory and chop the watercress, discarding the ends of the stalks. Slice the salami and the cheese into matchstick strips. Put all the salad ingredients, salami, anchovy fillets, and cheese into a salad bowl. Put the remaining ingredients into a screw-topped jar and shake well. Pour over the salad, toss, and chill for 30 minutes before serving.

Japanese Pickled Lettuce, Cucumber, and Turnip
Serves 4

2 lettuce hearts
1 cucumber

1 turnip
1 teaspoon salt

Cut the lettuces in quarters, wash and dry them thoroughly and put into a bowl. Peel the cucumber, cut into thirds, then cut into thin slices lengthways. Peel the turnip and cut into thin slices. Put the cucumber and turnip into the bowl with the lettuce and sprinkle over the salt. Cover the bowl and leave the vegetables in a cool place or refrigerator for 48 hours, turning the ingredients from time to time.

Crushed Wheat Salad
Serves 4

This Arabian vegetarian salad makes an interesting addition to a meal. Crushed wheat is called a variety of different names, such as burghul and kibble, but it is not difficult to obtain from health food stores.

4 oz/100g crushed wheat
2 tablespoons finely chopped
   shallots or spring onions
6 tablespoons chopped parsley
6 tablespoons chopped mint
2 tablespoons olive oil

2 tablespoons lemon juice
salt and freshly milled black pepper
To garnish:
black olives
2 tomatoes, sliced

Put the crushed wheat into a bowl and cover with cold water. Leave for 30 minutes

92

Smith Salad ▶

during which time it will expand. Drain, then wrap in a tea towel and wring out to remove as much moisture as possible. Put into a bowl and add the shallots or spring onions, parsely, mint, oil, and lemon juice. Season to taste with salt and pepper. Put the mixture into a shallow dish and garnish with black olives and tomatoes.

SAVOURY SALADS WITH FRUIT

Fruit, such as oranges and apples, is often used in conjunction with meat, such as pork and duck, to counteract the fattiness and richness, but it also blends very well with cheese and olives, as well as lettuce, cucumber, celery, etc. Some of the combinations may sound a little strange, but taste surprisingly good – I was very dubious when I came across the recipe for Raspberry Salad with Blue Cheese Dressing, but (rather nervously) served it as part of a mixed hors d'œuvre and was lucky to find a teaspoonful left for myself as everyone thought it was so good!

Elona Salad
Serves 4

1 medium-sized cucumber
8 oz/200g strawberries

salt and freshly milled black pepper
2 tablespoons dry white wine

Peel the cucumber and cut into thin slices. Hull the strawberries and cut into slices. Arrange the cucumber and strawberry slices attractively on a serving plate. Season with salt and pepper and pour over the wine. Cover and chill in the refrigerator for an hour before serving.

94

Australian Summer Salad
Serves 4

4 sticks celery
¼ cucumber
2 dessert apples

juice of 1 orange
1 small lettuce

Dice the celery and cucumber. Core the apples, peel if wished, and dice. Put into a bowl with the celery and cucumber, pour over the orange juice and toss well. Chill in the refrigerator for 1 hour. Wash and dry the lettuce, put into a polythene bag to crisp, and refrigerate for 1 hour. To serve, arrange the lettuce leaves on a serving plate and pile the diced vegetables, together with the juice, into the centre.

Caribbean Salad
Serves 6

1 small lettuce
1 medium-sized fresh pineapple
4 sticks celery
1 small green pepper

1 small red pepper
2 oz/50g walnuts
6 tablespoons mayonnaise
salt and freshly milled black pepper

Wash the lettuce, dry well and place in a polythene bag. Put into the refrigerator and leave to crisp for 1 hour. Peel the pineapple, cut into slices and remove the core, then dice. Chop the celery and chop the peppers, discarding the cores and seeds. Roughly chop the walnuts. Put the pineapple, celery, peppers, and walnuts into a bowl. Add the mayonnaise and blend well, then season to taste with salt and pepper. Just before serving, arrange the lettuce leaves round the outside of a salad bowl and spoon the pineapple mixture into the centre.

Greek Orange and Olive Salad
Serves 4–6

4 large oranges
4 oz/100g Greek black olives
1 tablespoon finely chopped onion
4 tablespoons olive oil

2 tablespoons lemon juice
pinch dry mustard
salt and freshly milled black pepper

Peel the oranges, discarding all the white pith and skin, and cut into segments; do this over a basin so that you can catch any juice. Stone the olives. Put the orange segments, olives, and onion into a salad bowl. Put all the remaining ingredients, including any orange juice, into a screw-topped jar and shake until well blended. Pour over the oranges and olives and toss well. Chill for an hour before serving.

Orange and Watercress Salad
Serves 4–6

A watercress and orange salad tossed in a French dressing is traditionally served with roast duck. This salad has a mild curry dressing on it and can be served with a variety of dishes.

1 large bunch watercress
2 oranges
4 tablespoons olive oil
1 tablespoon wine vinegar
1 tablespoon lemon juice

2 teaspoons curry powder (see
  method)
salt and freshly milled black pepper
1 teaspoon finely chopped shallots

Wash the watercress, trim off the stalks and place in a polythene bag in the refrigerator for at least 1 hour to crisp. Peel the oranges, discarding all the skin and pith, and cut into segments. Chill. Put the olive oil, vinegar, lemon juice, curry powder, seasoning, and shallots into a screw-topped jar. Shake until well blended. The exact quantity of curry powder needed will depend on the strength of your particular brand. Just before serving arrange the watercress and orange segments in a salad bowl, pour over the dressing and mix well.

Orange and Cauliflower Salad
Serves 6

1 small cauliflower
2 oranges
2 sticks celery
1 small onion
1 apple

8 oz/200g Edam cheese
juice of 2 lemons
grated rind 1 lemon
2 teaspoons chopped mint
salt and freshly milled black pepper

Break the cauliflower into florets, peel the oranges, discarding all the white pith, and cut into segments. Chop the celery and onion and peel and grate the apple. Put all the fruit and vegetables into a serving bowl with the cheese, which can be either diced or cut into thin slices. Put the remaining ingredients into a screw-topped jar and shake until they are well blended. Pour over the salad, toss well and leave for 30 minutes before serving.

Fruited Cabbage Salad
For a party, this salad can look very attractive if it is served in a scooped-out red cabbage. Cut off any very coarse outer leaves, trim the base of the cabbage so that it stands upright, then cut a slice off the top. Scoop out the inside of the cabbage using a sharp knife and leaving a $\frac{1}{4}$ in/0.75cm thick layer of leaves for the shell.

Serves 6

1 lb/400g red cabbage
1 green pepper
$\frac{1}{2}$ small pineapple
1 grapefruit
1 turnip or kohlrabi, peeled and grated
2 shallots or 6 spring onions, finely
  chopped

3 sticks celery, finely chopped
3 oz/75g hazelnuts, coarsely
  chopped
generous $\frac{1}{4}$ pint/150ml mayonnaise
salt and freshly milled black pepper

Finely shred the cabbage, discarding any tough outer leaves and stalks. Chop the pepper, discarding the core and seeds. Peel the pineapple and chop very finely.

Peel the grapefruit, removing all the white pith and cut into pieces, discarding any pith. Put all the fruit, vegetables and nuts into a bowl. Add the mayonnaise and blend well. Season to taste.

Miami Salad
Serves 4

1 lettuce
2 tangerines
2 tomatoes, sliced

4 slices of lemon
1 tablespoon olive oil
salt and freshly milled black pepper

Wash the lettuce and dry well. Put into a polythene bag in the refrigerator to crisp for 1 hour. Place the lettuce leaves on four individual plates. Peel the tangerines, discarding all the white pith, and cut into segments. Arrange the tangerine segments, tomato, and lemon slices on the lettuce leaves. Sprinkle over the oil and season with salt and pepper.

Banana Creole Salad
Serves 4

1 small lettuce
1 large orange
2 large bananas
1 tablespoon chopped nuts

2 tablespoons lightly whipped
 double cream
4 tablespoons mayonnaise

Wash the lettuce, dry well, put into a polythene bag and leave to crisp for 1 hour in the refrigerator. Arrange the lettuce leaves on four individual plates. Peel the orange, discarding all the white pith, and cut into segments; do this over a basin to catch the juice. Peel the bananas, cut into thick slices, then toss with the orange segments and orange juice in the basin. Spoon the orange and bananas on to the lettuce. Fold the cream into the mayonnaise, then spread over the fruit. Sprinkle with the chopped nuts before serving.

Pears with Cream Cheese Balls
Serves 4

8 oz/200g cream cheese
2 teaspoons finely chopped celery
few drops Tabasco sauce
salt
2 oz/50g hazelnuts, finely chopped

4 ripe dessert pears
1 tablespoon lemon juice
To garnish:
few crisp lettuce leaves

Sieve the cream cheese, then add the celery and Tabasco and season to taste with salt. Form the cream cheese into small balls and roll in the finely chopped nuts. Peel the pears, cut them in half and remove the cores with a teaspoon, then brush them with lemon juice to preserve the colour. Arrange the pears on a serving plate with the cut side uppermost and pile the cheese balls on top. Garnish the dish with crisp lettuce leaves.

97

Roquefort Pear Salad
Serves 4

4 ripe dessert pears
lemon juice (see method)
2 oz/50g Roquefort or other blue
   cheese
2 oz/50g cream cheese
2 tablespoons mayonnaise
1 tablespoon chopped walnuts

a little single cream or top of the
   milk (see method)
salt and freshly milled black pepper
To garnish:
lettuce leaves
paprika

Peel and halve the pears, scoop out the cores with a spoon and dip the fruit quickly in lemon juice to preserve its colour. Place on a serving dish. Mash the Roquefort or other blue cheese with the cream cheese and mayonnaise. Add the walnuts, then soften the dressing with sufficient cream or milk to give a good coating consistency. Season to taste and spoon the dressing over the pears. Garnish with a few crisp lettuce leaves and sprinkle with paprika just before serving.

Stuffed Peaches with Cheese
Serves 6

3 large peaches
tarragon vinegar or lemon juice (see
   method)
1 oz/25g butter
3 oz/75g Cheddar cheese, finely
   grated
2 tablespoons grated Parmesan
   cheese
salt

pinch cayenne pepper
3 oz/75g Demi-sel or other soft
   cream cheese
$\frac{1}{4}$ pint/125ml single cream
To garnish:
few crisp lettuce leaves
2 tomatoes, sliced and/or $\frac{1}{2}$ box
   mustard and cress
paprika

Peel the peaches. If they are difficult to peel, put into a bowl, cover with boiling water and leave for 1 minute, then drain and peel as you would tomatoes. Cut them in half and take out the stones. Brush the peaches with a very little tarragon vinegar or lemon juice to preserve the colour. Cream the butter, beat in the Cheddar and Parmesan cheese and season with salt and cayenne pepper. Form into six balls and use to fill the hollows in the peaches where the stones were removed. Arrange a stuffed peach, a few crisp lettuce leaves, tomato slices, and/or mustard and cress on each of six plates. Beat the Demi-sel or other cream cheese and beat in the cream to give a good coating consistency. Spoon over the peaches just before serving and sprinkle with the paprika.

Raspberry Salad with Blue Cheese Dressing
Serves 3–4

2 oz/50g Danish Blue cheese, finely
   crumbled
4 tablespoons mayonnaise

8 oz/200g fresh raspberries
salt and freshly milled black pepper
$\frac{1}{4}$ cucumber, thinly sliced

98

Roquefort Pear Salad ▶

Stir the cheese into the mayonnaise and blend well, then carefully fold in the raspberries, so that you don't break them. Add seasoning to taste, if necessary. Arrange the sliced cucumber round the edge of a serving plate and pile the raspberry mixture into the centre.

Strawberry and Yogurt Salad
Serves 4

12 oz/300g strawberries
2 tablespoons lemon juice
¼ pint/125ml natural yogurt

1 clove garlic, crushed
salt and freshly milled black pepper

Hull the strawberries, cut into halves if small, or quarters if large and put into a serving bowl. In a basin blend the lemon juice into the yogurt and add the garlic and seasoning. Pour over the strawberries and toss well.

VEGETABLE SOUPS AND COCKTAILS

Iced vegetable soups make a delicious starter to a meal and so can vegetable juices. At one time anyone who drank vegetable juices was thought of as a Health Food fanatic, but canned vegetable juices can now be bought in many supermarkets and with a blender they are very easy to make in your own home. They are also marvellous for slimmers as they provide valuable nutrients without adding too many calories and can make a refreshing drink during the day, especially in hot weather.

100

Iced Tomato Soup
Serves 4

2 lb/800g tomatoes
2 sticks celery
1 small bunch spring onions

½ pint/250ml water
pinch sugar
salt and freshly milled black pepper

Peel the tomatoes and roughly chop the celery. Clean the spring onions, chop 2 tablespoons of the green part to reserve for the garnish and roughly chop the remainder. Put the tomatoes, celery, spring onions, and water into a blender and blend until smooth. Add the sugar and season to taste with salt and pepper. Chill the soup for at least 4 hours before serving, until it is very cold, and sprinkle with the chopped spring onions.

Gazpacho Andaluz
Serves 6

To the purist this recipe may not be strictly raw as it contains breadcrumbs and chicken stock, but it is *so* good I felt it had to be included.

1 green pepper
2 lb/800g tomatoes, peeled
2 cloves garlic
1 medium-sized onion, peeled
½ cucumber, peeled

2 oz/50g fresh white or brown
   breadcrumbs
2 tablespoons red wine vinegar
¼ pint/125ml chicken stock
6 tablespoons olive oil
salt and freshly milled black pepper

Core the pepper and discard the seeds. Put it with the tomatoes, garlic, onion, and cucumber into a blender and blend until smooth. Alternatively, chop the pepper, onion, and cucumber very finely, rub the tomatoes through a sieve and crush the garlic. Add the breadcrumbs, vinegar, stock, and oil and season to taste. Chill for at least 4 hours. Add a few ice cubes to the soup just before serving and serve with finely chopped raw onion, cucumber, and pepper as accompaniments.

Iced Cucumber Soup
Serves 4–6

There are many variations of this Middle Eastern soup, but this one is particularly simple to prepare.

1 large cucumber
½ pint/250ml single cream
¼ pint/125ml natural yogurt
1 clove garlic, crushed
2 tablespoons vinegar

salt and freshly milled black pepper
2 tablespoons chopped mint
To garnish:
sprigs of mint

Wipe the cucumber, but do not peel it. Grate it coarsely into a bowl, and stir in the cream, yogurt, garlic, vinegar, seasoning, and mint. Turn into a serving bowl and chill in the refrigerator for at least 1 hour. Taste and adjust the seasoning when the flavours have infused and garnish with sprigs of mint before serving.

Iced Avocado Soup
Serves 4

2 ripe avocado pears
juice of ½ lemon
10 oz/283g can consommé

¼ pint/125ml soured cream
salt and freshly milled black pepper

Cut the avocado pears in half and cut 4 slices for decoration. Dip these in lemon juice to preserve the colour. Remove the stones from the avocado pears and put on one side. Sieve the flesh and mix with the remaining ingredients or purée all the ingredients in a blender. Mix well, taste and adjust the seasoning. Turn into a serving dish, add the stones (this helps prevent the soup from discolouring) and chill for about 1 hour. It is not a good idea to make this soup more than 3–4 hours before you want to serve it as it tends to discolour. Garnish with the reserved slices of avocado before serving.

Tomato Ice
Serves 4

A refreshing starter, and a good way of preserving tomatoes.

2 lb/800g tomatoes
1 small onion
3 sprigs marjoram
juice of 1 lemon

salt and freshly milled black pepper
2 teaspoons sugar (see method)
To garnish:
sprigs of mint

Peel the tomatoes and onion and chop roughly. Put into a blender with the majoram and lemon juice and blend to a smooth purée. Season with salt and pepper and add sugar to taste. Turn into a freezing container and freeze for 4 hours or until solid. Remove from the freezer and leave at room temperature for about 15 minutes before serving or in a refrigerator for 30–45 minutes. Turn out of the container and crush the ice with a rolling pin. Pile the crystals into individual glasses, garnish with mint and serve as soon as possible.

Russian Fresh Berry Soup
Serves 4

Fruit soups are a traditional feature of Russian and Balkan cookery. They are sometimes served hot, but it is more usual to serve them iced.

1 lb/800g fresh raspberries,
  blackberries, ripe gooseberries, or
  blackcurrants
4 egg yolks
2–4 oz/50–100g caster sugar (see
  method)

¼ pint/125ml water
¼ pint/125ml double cream
To garnish:
2 tablespoons chopped chives

Wash and sieve the berries or put them into a blender to make a smooth purée. Blend the egg yolks with the sugar and a third of the fruit purée in the top of a double saucepan or in a bowl which can be put over a pan of hot water. The amount of sugar used will depend on the type and sweetness of the fruit, but the soup should not be over-sweetened or it will become more like a dessert. Put the saucepan or bowl over a pan of gently simmering water and allow the mixture to thicken, stirring all the time. Remove from the heat and stir in the remaining fruit purée, the water, and almost all the cream. Chill for at least 6 hours before serving as it should be served very cold. Just before serving pour over the remaining cream to make a pattern and sprinkle with the chopped chives.

Pineapple and Vegetable Cocktail
Serves 4

1 small carrot
1 stick celery
1/4 cucumber
3/4 pint/375ml chilled unsweetened
    pineapple juice

few ice cubes
To garnish:
4 slices lemon

Peel or scrape the carrot and chop roughly. Roughly chop the celery and peel and roughly chop the cucumber. Put all the ingredients, except the ice, into a blender and blend until smooth, then add the ice and blend for a few seconds until lightly crushed. Pour into glasses and garnish each one with a slice of lemon.

Mixed Vegetable Cocktail
Serves 1–2

1 carrot
1 tomato
1 small stick celery
1 tablespoon chopped parsley

salt and freshly milled black pepper
juice of 1/2 lemon
1/4 pint/125ml water
1 teaspoon yeast extract

Peel the carrot and tomato and chop roughly with the celery. Put into a blender with all the remaining ingredients and blend until smooth. The cocktail is best if served well chilled, so either chill after preparing or replace the water with crushed ice before blending.

Tomato Juice
Serves 2–3

1 lb tomatoes
1/2 teaspoon sugar

salt and freshly milled black pepper
few drops Worcestershire sauce
    (optional)

Peel the tomatoes. Put into a blender and blend until smooth. Add the sugar and season to taste with salt and pepper and a little Worcestershire sauce, if liked. Pour into glasses and add a couple of ice cubes to each one.

103

VEGETABLE SAUCES

Fresh Cucumber Relish
Serves 6

This is a particularly good slimmer's sauce for cold meats.

1 small onion
1 carrot
$\frac{1}{2}$ large cucumber
1 clove garlic (optional)

2 tablespoons distilled malt vinegar
$\frac{1}{2}$ teaspoon dill seed
salt and freshly milled black pepper

Peel and roughly chop the onion, carrot, and cucumber. Put the onion and carrot into a blender with the garlic and vinegar and blend until smooth. Add the cucumber, dill, and seasoning and blend for a few seconds to break up the cucumber, but it should not be too smooth. Leave the mixture for 15 minutes, then strain it. Taste and adjust the seasoning of the relish and chill lightly before serving. *Note*: Do not discard the liquid as this is full of vitamins and makes a refreshing drink if well chilled.

Celery and Onion Relish
Serves 4–6

1 small head of celery
1 small onion

salt and freshly milled black pepper
1 teaspoon chopped tarragon

Wash the celery and discard any very tough outer stalks. Put the celery stalks and the onion through a mincer. Add the salt and pepper and tarragon and leave for an hour before serving for the flavours to infuse.

104

Ravigote Sauce
Serves 4

Serve this sauce with salami or other cold meats.

½ bunch watercress
1 tablespoon chopped parsley
1 tablespoon chopped chives
1 tablespoon chopped tarragon
1 tablespoon chopped chervil
1 clove garlic, crushed

3 anchovy fillets (optional)
2 tablespoons wine vinegar
½ teaspoon French mustard
¼ pint/125ml olive oil
freshly milled black pepper
salt, if necessary

Wash and chop the watercress, discarding the stalks. Either put all the ingredients into a blender and purée them, or pound the watercress with the herbs, garlic, and anchovy fillets until you have a smooth paste. Then gradually add the vinegar, mustard, oil, and pepper. If you have used the anchovy fillets, you will probably find that the sauce does not need any salt, but taste and adjust the seasoning accordingly.

Tomato Sauce with Basil
Serves 4–6

1 lb/400g tomatoes
2 teaspoons red wine vinegar

1 teaspoon chopped basil
salt and freshly milled black pepper

Peel the tomatoes and discard the cores and pips. Sieve or put into a blender until smooth. Add the vinegar and basil and season to taste.

Indian Mint Chutney
Serves 4–6

This is a typical recipe for the kind of chutney which the Indians prepare freshly for each meal.

2 oz/50g fresh mint leaves
8 spring onions
2 small fresh green chillies
salt

1 teaspoon sugar
1 teaspoon garam masala
1 tablespoon pomegranate seeds
1 tablespoon lime juice

Wash and drain the mint leaves, then chop them finely. Finely chop the spring onions and the chillies. Put these into a mortar and pound with a little salt, the sugar, and garam masala. Crush the pomegranate seeds, add to the mixture and pound until smooth. Stir in the lime juice and turn into a serving bowl.

Greek Lime Sauce
Serves 6

This sauce makes a pleasant alternative to French dressing.

¼ pint/125ml fresh lime juice
¼ pint/125ml olive oil
¼ pint/125ml clear honey

salt
1 teaspoon paprika

Put the lime juice into a bowl, then gradually whisk in the olive oil. Add the honey, salt, and paprika and beat hard for 5 minutes. Alternatively make the sauce in a blender and blend at high speed for about 30 seconds.

Walnut Sauce
Serves 4

This sauce can be served either as an hors d'œuvre with fresh bread and sticks of celery to dip into it or as an accompaniment to cold meats.

3 oz/75g shelled walnuts
2 cloves garlic

$\frac{1}{4}$ pint/125ml olive oil
salt and freshly milled black pepper

Put the walnuts into a basin, cover with boiling water and leave for 2 minutes, then drain and skin them. Put into a mortar with the garlic and pound until smooth, or use a blender. Add the oil, a drop at a time at first, then more quickly until you have a smooth thick sauce. Season to taste with salt and pepper.

FRUIT

FRESH FRUIT is surely one of Nature's greatest gifts and now that fruit can be flown all over the world in a matter of hours, we are lucky enough to be able to enjoy it all through the year no matter where we live. It is also comforting to know that something that tastes so delicious is also good for you. 'An apple a day keeps the doctor away,' was the old saying, and if you add an orange as well you are getting near the truth.

I would put a number of the recipes in this chapter in the luxury class, but they are almost all very quick and simple to prepare and ideal if you are entertaining and have only a little time available for cooking. I have deliberately not included a set recipe for fruit salad as the constituents of this will vary enormously with the time of year and the fruit available. However, when making a fruit salad it is worthwhile spending a little time preparing the fruit well – de-pipping grapes, stoning cherries, segmenting oranges, etc, so that it is easy to eat.

Charoseth
Serves 2–3

2 dessert apples
2 tablespoons finely chopped
  blanched almonds

1 tablespoon chopped sultanas
$\frac{1}{4}$ teaspoon powdered cinnamon
sieved icing sugar

Peel the apples and grate them, discarding the cores. Put into a basin and blend in the almonds, sultanas, and cinnamon. Roll into small balls, then dust with icing sugar.

108

Avocado and Melon Cocktail
Serves 4–6

This makes a particularly refreshing starter to a meal. I have suggested just chopping the fruit, but if you prefer, you can cut it into balls using a special cutter.

1 large Charentais melon
2 avocado pears
2 tablespoons lemon or lime juice

1 thick slice watermelon (optional)
To garnish:
sprigs of mint

Cut the melon in half, scoop out the seeds and carefully chop the flesh into ½ inch/1.25cm pieces. Put into a bowl together with all the juice. Peel the avocado pears and slice the flesh. Toss lightly in lemon or lime juice to preserve the colour, then add to the melon in the bowl. Cut the watermelon in the same way as the Charentais melon; this is not essential but as well as adding flavour, adds colour to the cocktail. Toss all the ingredients lightly together, chill for about 30 minutes, then turn into individual glasses. Garnish each glass with a sprig of mint before serving.

Avocado Fool
Serves 4

This dessert should not be prepared more than about 3 hours before you wish to serve it as even with the lime juice the avocado pears tend to discolour. It should, however, be served lightly chilled so prepare at least 1 hour before serving.

2 large avocado pears
juice of 2 medium-sized limes
2 tablespoons icing sugar (see method)

2 tablespoons brandy
¼ pint/125ml double cream
To decorate:
1 lime, thinly sliced

Peel the avocado pears and put into a blender with the lime juice and sugar. Blend until you have a smooth purée. Add the brandy. Whip the cream until it is just thick, then fold in the avocado purée. Taste and add a little more sugar if necessary, then turn into a serving bowl or individual glasses. Decorate with twists of lime before serving.

South African Banana Fool
Serves 6

8 bananas
3 eggs, separated
2 tablespoons brandy or rum

2 oz/50g caster sugar
¼ pint/125ml double cream
¼ teaspoon grated nutmeg

Mash the bananas into a smooth pulp, then beat in the egg yolks, the brandy or rum, and three-quarters of the sugar. Whisk the egg whites until they form stiff peaks, then fold half of them into the banana pulp. Turn into a serving bowl. Lightly whip the cream and spread this over the top of the banana mixture. Gradually whisk the remaining sugar into the remaining whisked egg white, spread this over the top of the whipped cream and sprinkle with the grated nutmeg. Serve as soon as possible to avoid discoloration of the fruit.

Banana Cheese
Serves 4

3 ripe bananas
2 tablespoons lemon juice
4 oz/100g fresh cream cheese

2–3 tablespoons single cream or top
of the milk
2 tablespoons caster sugar

Peel and mash the bananas and add the lemon juice. Beat the cream cheese with
the cream or top of the milk and sugar, then stir in the bananas. Blend well and turn
into four small individual serving dishes.
Variation: This dessert becomes 'extra special' if you add 2 tablespoons of white or
brown rum to it.

Banana and Walnut Dessert
Serves 4–6

4 large ripe bananas
juice of ½ lemon
4 oz/100g caster sugar
2 oz/50g walnuts, chopped

½ pint/250ml natural yogurt
To decorate:
walnut halves

Mash the peeled bananas with a fork. Add the remaining ingredients and mix well,
then turn into a serving bowl and decorate with the walnut halves. Chill for at least
1 hour before serving.
Variations: Use hazelnuts instead of walnuts and/or replace half the yogurt with
whipped double cream.

Bananas in Red Wine
Serves 4

½ pint/250ml red wine
4 oz/100g sugar
¼ teaspoon ground ginger
1 inch/2.5cm piece cinnamon

2 cloves
4 large bananas
To serve:
whipped cream

Put the wine, sugar, ginger, cinnamon, and cloves into a saucepan. Bring slowly to
the boil and simmer for 5 minutes, then strain. Peel the bananas and cut into thick
slices. Put into a serving dish and pour over the warm, but not hot, wine. Chill for at
least 2 hours in the refrigerator before serving with whipped cream.

Fresh Figs and Yogurt
Serves 4

8 ripe figs,
¼ pint/125ml double cream

¼ pint/125ml natural yogurt
3 tablespoons soft brown sugar

Put the figs into a large bowl. Cover with hot water, leave for 1 minute, then drain
and peel as you would tomatoes. Slice each fig into four pieces. Whip the cream
until it just holds its shape, then stir in the yogurt and blend well. Put a quarter of

the cream mixture into the bottom of a glass serving dish, cover with a third of the figs and continue these layers, ending with a layer of cream and sprinkling each layer with a little of the sugar. Chill in the refrigerator for at least 2 hours before serving so that the sugar melts into the cream.

Variation: This method is also good for small seedless grapes. Replace the figs with 12 oz/300g seedless grapes and make as above.

Melons with Raspberry Purée
Serves 4

2 Charantais or Ogen melons
8 oz/200g raspberries
2 oz/50g cream cheese
2 oz/50g caster sugar

$\frac{1}{4}$ pint/125ml double cream
1 tablespoon Framboise liqueur, kirsch, or brandy

Cut the melons in half crossways and remove the seeds. Sieve the raspberries, reserving a few for decoration, or put into a blender to make a smooth purée. Beat the cream cheese with the sugar, then gradually beat in the raspberry purée. Lightly whip the cream until it just holds its shape, then fold into the raspberry and cream mixture. Spoon into the centre of the melons and decorate with the reserved raspberries. Chill for 1 hour before serving.

Guyanan Watermelon
Serves 6–8

1 watermelon, about 3 lb/1.2 kilos in weight
3 tablespoons icing sugar

$\frac{1}{4}$ pint/125ml rum
3 oranges

Cut a slice off the top of the melon. Scoop the melon out, using a melon-baller, or scoop out and cut into chunks, but keep the skin of the melon intact. Put the balls or chunks into a bowl, sprinkle with the sugar and pour in the rum. Peel the oranges, discarding all the white pith, then cut into segments. Add to the melon mixture, then pile back into the melon case. Chill for 1 hour in the refrigerator before serving.

Fresh Orange Jelly
Serves 4

3 large oranges
1 lemon
water (see method)

$\frac{1}{2}$ oz/15g powdered gelatine
sugar to taste

Peel the oranges and lemon thinly, removing only the rind and leaving the white pith. Put the rind into a saucepan with $\frac{1}{2}$ pint/250ml water. Bring to the boil and simmer gently for 10 minutes to extract the flavour. Put 4 tablespoons of cold water into a basin, sprinkle over the gelatine and leave to soften for 5 minutes. Remove the pan containing the orange and lemon rind from the heat. Add the

softened gelatine, stir until it has dissolved, then strain into a measuring jug. Squeeze the juice from the oranges and lemon and strain into the jug. The fruit juice and gelatine mixture should make up to 1 pint/500ml, but if necessary make up the quantity with cold water. Add sugar to taste, stir until it has dissolved, then turn into a mould or dish and chill until set.

Orange Sorbet
Serves 4

This quickly made sorbet uses a can of concentrated frozen orange juice, and could easily be made with grapefruit juice as well.

2 oz/50g sugar
$\frac{1}{2}$ pint/250ml water plus 4 tablespoons
2 teaspoons gelatine

$6\frac{1}{4}$ oz/178g can concentrated frozen
   orange juice
1 egg white

Dissolve the sugar in the $\frac{1}{2}$ pint/250ml water and allow to cool. Sprinkle the gelatine over the 4 tablespoons water in a basin and leave to soften for 5 minutes. Stand the basin over a pan of hot water and leave until the gelatine has dissolved. Add to the sugar syrup with the thawed, but undiluted, orange juice. Mix well, pour into a container and freeze for 1 hour or until almost firm. Remove from the container and mash the sorbet so that no large lumps remain. Whisk the egg white until stiff and fold into the sorbet. Return to the container, cover and freeze for at least 3 hours.

Marinated Oranges
Serves 4

6 medium-sized oranges
4 oz/100g caster sugar

4 tablespoons Cointreau, Grand
   Marnier, or Curaçao

Peel one of the oranges thinly, removing only the rind and leaving the white pith. Cut into very thin shreds and put into a basin. Cover with boiling water and leave for 5 minutes, then drain. Peel all the oranges with a sharp knife, discarding all the white pith, then cut into slices. Put into a serving dish and sprinkle over the sugar. Leave for 5 minutes for the sugar to dissolve, then stir in the liqueur. Chill in the refrigerator for at least 1 hour. Decorate with the shreds of orange rind before serving.

Passion Fruit Cream
Serves 6–8

2 tablespoons water
2 teaspoons powdered gelatine
$\frac{1}{2}$ pint/250ml passion fruit pulp
  (about 12 passion fruit)

juice of 1 lemon
2 oz/50g caster sugar
$\frac{1}{2}$ pint/250ml double cream
$\frac{1}{4}$ pint/125ml single cream

◀ Melons with Raspberry Purée

Put the water into a basin, sprinkle over the gelatine and leave to soften for 5 minutes. Stand the basin over a pan of gently simmering water and leave until the gelatine has dissolved. Tip the passion fruit pulp into a bowl and stir in the gelatine, lemon juice, and sugar. Blend well and put on one side until the mixture is beginning to set. Whip the double and single cream together until it holds its shape. Fold in the passion fruit mixture, then turn into a serving bowl and chill for 2 hours until set.

Variation: This typical Australian dessert can also be served as an ice cream; simply freeze it for 3–4 hours.

Peaches and Grapes in Crème de Menthe
Serves 4–6

4 ripe peaches
1 lb/400g seedless green grapes
6 oz/150g sugar

3 tablespoons white or
   green Crème de Menthe

Peel the peaches and slice them thinly. If the skins are difficult to remove pour boiling water over the fruit, leave for one minute, then drain and peel. Place the sliced peaches in a basin. Wash the grapes, remove the stems, and add the grapes to the peaches. Add the sugar and Crème de Menthe and mix well. Pack the fruit into a large screw-topped jar or other container and refrigerate for at least 24 hours before serving.

Peaches with Raspberry Sauce
Serves 4

4 ripe peaches
1 tablespoon lemon juice
8 oz/200g raspberries
1–2 oz/25–50g caster sugar

2 tablespoons white wine
1 tablespoon Framboise liqueur
   (optional)

Skin the peaches (see above), cut them in half and place on four individual serving plates. Brush with a little lemon juice to prevent them from browning. Sieve the raspberries or purée in a blender with the sugar, wine and liqueur, if using. Pour over the peaches and chill for 1 hour before serving.

Peach Whip
Serves 6

4 ripe peaches
little lemon juice (see method)
¼ pint/125ml double cream

2 egg whites
3 oz/75g caster sugar

Peel the peaches; if they are difficult to peel, put them into a bowl, cover with boiling water for 1 minute, then drain and peel as you would tomatoes. Halve the peaches and remove the stones. Cut 6 good slices of peach for decoration and dip these quickly in a very little lemon juice to preserve the colour. Sieve the remaining peaches or purée in a blender. Lightly whip the cream until it just holds its shape,

114

then fold into the peach purée. Whisk the egg whites until they form stiff peaks, then gradually beat in the sugar, a teaspoon at a time. Fold the egg whites into the peach and cream purée. Pile into six glasses and decorate with the reserved slices of peach before serving.

Peaches in Red Wine
Serves 4

This dish should not be prepared too long before serving or the peaches will become rather soggy. If you want to serve it chilled, prepare just before serving, but chill the wine for a few hours in the refrigerator beforehand. Nectarines are delicious, prepared in the same way but you will need about 8 medium-sized ones for four people.

4 large peaches	$\frac{1}{2}$ pint/250ml red wine
2 tablespoons caster sugar	

Peel the peaches: if you cannot do this easily with a knife, cover with boiling water for 1 minute, then drain and peel. Cut into slices and place in four individual glasses. Sprinkle with the sugar and pour over the wine.

Shredded Pineapple
Serves 4–6

1 medium-sized ripe pineapple	$\frac{1}{2}$ pint/250ml double cream
4 oz/100g caster sugar	

Peel the pineapple and remove all the eyes, then grate it coarsely. It is a good idea to do this on a large plate so that you do not waste any of the juice which comes out of the pineapple. Turn into a bowl, add the sugar and stir until the sugar has dissolved. Whip the cream until it just holds its shape, then fold into the pineapple mixture. Turn into one large bowl or into individual glasses and chill for at least 2 hours before serving.
Variation: For an added touch of luxury, add 2 tablespoons of kirsch with the sugar.

Fresh Raspberry Ice Cream
Serves 4

1 lb/400g raspberries	$\frac{1}{4}$ pint/125ml double cream, lightly
sieved icing sugar (see method)	whipped
2 eggs, separated	

Sieve the raspberries or put into a blender. Sweeten to taste with icing sugar. Beat the egg yolks and 1 oz/25g icing sugar until thick and creamy. Whisk the egg whites until they form stiff peaks, then gradually beat in 2 oz/50g icing sugar, a teaspoon at a time. Gradually whisk the egg-yolk mixture into this, then fold in the raspberry purée and cream. Turn into a container and freeze for at least 4 hours.

115

Raspberry and Yogurt Ice
Serves 6

8 oz/200g raspberries
2–3 oz/50–75 caster sugar
juice of ½ lemon
½ pint/250ml natural yogurt

2 tablespoons water
2 teaspoons powdered gelatine
2 egg whites

Put the raspberries, sugar, and lemon juice into a blender, purée, then stir in the yogurt. Put the water into a basin. Sprinkle over the gelatine and leave to soften for 5 minutes. Stand the basin over a pan of gently simmering water and leave until the gelatine has dissolved, then stir into the raspberry mixture. Turn into a container and freeze until the mixture is just beginning to set. Remove from the freezer, turn into a cold basin and beat until all the ice crystals have been removed and the mixture is smooth. Whisk the egg whites until they form soft peaks, then fold them into the raspberry mixture. Spoon back into the container, cover and freeze until firm, about 4 hours.

Marinated Redcurrants
Serves 4

1 lb/400g redcurrants
juice of 2 large oranges

4 oz/100g caster sugar

Remove the currants from the sprigs and place in a serving dish. Pour over the orange juice and sprinkle with the sugar. Cover and put into the refrigerator to marinate for 6 hours before serving.
Variations:
Use half blackcurrants and half redcurrants
Add 2 tablespoons white wine or liqueur.

Strawberries Romanoff
Serves 4

1 lb/400g fresh strawberries
3 tablespoons icing sugar
2 tablespoons white rum

¼ pint/125ml double cream
2 tablespoons kirsch

Hull the strawberries and place in a bowl. Sprinkle over 2 tablespoons of the sugar and all the rum and toss well. Cover and chill in the refrigerator for at least 45 minutes. One hour before serving, whip the cream until it is stiff, then add the remaining sugar and the kirsch. Stir in the strawberries and toss well together. Turn into a serving dish, cover and chill until ready to serve.

Simple Strawberry Ice Cream
Serves 4

8 oz/200g strawberries
3 oz/75g icing sugar
1 tablespoon lemon juice

¼ pint/125ml double cream
¼ pint/125ml single cream

Hull the strawberries and cut them into small pieces. Put into a blender with the sugar and lemon juice and blend until smooth. Whip the double and single cream together until it holds its shape then fold in the strawberry purée. Turn into a container, cover and freeze for at least 4 hours. Serve the ice cream topped with fresh strawberries if wished.

Fraises en Vasque
Serves 4

1 lb/400g fresh strawberries
2 tablespoons sugar
2 tablespoons cherry brandy

¼ pint/125ml double cream
¼ pint/125ml soured cream
1 oz slivered almonds

Hull the strawberries and cut in half. Place them in a glass serving bowl and sprinkle them with the sugar and cherry brandy. Chill thoroughly. Whisk the double cream until it thickens but do not whip it. Blend in the soured cream. Pour over the strawberries and sprinkle with the slivered almonds. Serve immediately.

German Strawberry Bowl
Serves 4–6

1½ lb/600g strawberries
4 oz/100g caster sugar

2 tablespoons lemon juice
¼ pint/125ml light sweet white wine

Divide the strawberries into two equal portions, reserving the best fruit, and sprinkle them with half the sugar. Mash the remaining strawberries with the lemon juice and the other half of the sugar until you have a smooth purée, or use a blender. Add the wine, then pour this sauce over the whole berries. Stir well together, then turn into a serving bowl or into individual glasses or dishes. Chill lightly before serving.

Strawberry Water Ice
Serves 4

8 oz/200g strawberries
2 tablespoons icing sugar

bottled lemonade (see method)
2 egg whites

Hull the strawberries and cut into small pieces. Put into a blender with the sugar and blend until smooth. Measure the strawberry purée and make up to ¾ pint/375ml with lemonade. Turn into a freezing tray, cover and freeze until the mixture is beginning to freeze round the sides of the container. Remove from the freezer, turn into a cold basin and beat well to break up the ice crystals. Whip the egg whites until they form soft peaks, then fold into the strawberry mixture. Return to the freezing container, cover and freeze for at least 2 hours or until firm.
Note: If you wish to store the water ice for several days, it is advisable to add 2 teaspoons of gelatine dissolved in 2 tablespoons water to prevent the formation of ice crystals. Add this to the strawberry purée with the lemonade.

117

Strawberry and Orange Frost

Serves 2–3

8 oz/200g strawberries
½ pint/250ml fresh orange juice

1 tablespoon sugar
a few ice cubes

Put all the ingredients into a blender and blend until smooth. Pour into glasses and serve at once.

DRIED FRUIT AND NUTS

Dried fruit, and in particular prunes, have nasty connotations for many people. This is unfortunate, because in addition to their known function as a laxative, they are very rich in iron and Vitamin B. As with many other ingredients, the best tend to be expensive, but the plump dried figs, prunes, apricots, and dates which can be bought from good grocers and health food stores are delicious to eat just as they are, or they can be soaked and used in any number of ways. Nuts are another valuable food and provide vegetarians, and especially vegans (people who do not eat any animal products, such as eggs or cheese) with much of their daily requirements of protein and fat. Freshly cracked nuts do seem to have a flavour all their own, but if you require a quantity for a recipe, it is more practicable to use the packets of shelled nuts which are easily available all the year round.

Khoshaf (Syrian Fruit Salad)

Serves 4

This refreshing salad of dried fruits must be prepared 2 days before you wish to eat it so that all the fruits become sufficiently softened. Pine nuts are always added in

118

Syria, but as these are very expensive I have made them optional and they could be replaced by more almonds or walnuts. If you would like the salad a little sweeter, you can also add a little sugar dissolved in hot water.

2 oz/50g prunes
2 oz/50g dried apricots
2 oz/50g dried figs
2 tablespoons raisins

2 tablespoons blanched almonds
2 tablespoons shelled walnuts
2 tablespoons pine nuts (optional)
1 tablespoon rose water

Put the dried fruits into a bowl, cover with cold water and put into a cool place or refrigerator for 48 hours. Stir in the nuts and rose water and chill before serving.

Apricot and Yogurt Fool
Serves 4

8 oz/200g dried apricots
½ pint/250ml water
juice of 1 lemon

1 oz/25g brown sugar
¼ pint/125ml natural yogurt
1 oz/25g walnuts, finely chopped

Soak the apricots in the water and lemon juice for 24 hours until very soft. Put into a blender with the sugar and blend until smooth, or sieve. Blend the apricot purée with the yogurt. Turn into 4 individual glasses and chill for 2 hours. Sprinkle with the chopped walnuts before serving.

Prunes in White Wine
Serves 4

The tenderized California prunes, which are now widely available, do not require hours of soaking and long slow cooking in order to make them tender, and the large ones in particular are very good eaten just as they are. This dessert is simple to prepare and quite delicious, especially if it is served well chilled.

2 oz/50g sugar
grated rind and juice 1 orange

½ pint/250ml white wine
8 oz/200g tenderized prunes

Put the sugar, orange rind and juice, and wine into a bowl and leave for 10 minutes, stirring occasionally until the sugar has dissolved. Add the prunes, cover and put into the refrigerator for 12 hours.

Stuffed Prunes

The large, tenderized prunes make excellent little snacks to serve with drinks, or to hand round at the end of a meal. First remove the stones, keeping the fruit as whole as possible. The place where the stone has been removed can then be filled with a blanched almond and/or a piece of marzipan, some fondant icing, an anchovy fillet or a small piece of salt herring, or a small piece of salami or Parma ham, etc.

119

Muesli
Serves 4–6

Muesli originated in Switzerland where it is served as a dessert, but in the last few years an enormous number of commercially made products have come on the market, most of them being sold as breakfast cereals. The quality of these products varies enormously, some of them being good reproductions of the original Swiss version, but these on the whole are fairly expensive and it is not difficult and a lot cheaper to make your own. The basic grains used can be varied to suit individual tastes and can consist of a mixture of wheat meal, wheat flakes, oat flakes, maize meal, rye flakes, and bran, all of which can be obtained from health food stores. The following is a basic recipe which you can adapt as you wish by changing the grains, adding fresh fruit and increasing the quantities of nuts and dried fruit.

8 oz/200g mixed grains (see above)
2 tablespoons chopped mixed nuts,
  hazelnuts, almonds, walnuts
2 tablespoons raisins

2 tablespoons chopped dried apple
  and/or apricots
2 tablespoons brown or white sugar

Mix all the dry ingredients together and store in an airtight jar until required. To serve, add milk, yogurt, or fruit juice to taste.

Apple Muesli with Yogurt
Serves 4–6

2 dessert apples
2 tablespoons lemon juice
¼ pint/125ml natural yogurt
2 tablespoons honey

6 tablespoons water
4 oz/100g mixed grains (see above)
2 tablespoons chopped hazelnuts or
  almonds

Core the apples, peel if wished and chop finely. Put into a basin, pour over the lemon juice and mix well to prevent the apples from browning. Add the yogurt, honey and water and mix well, then stir in the mixed grains. Turn into a serving dish and sprinkle over the nuts.

120

Ingredients for Muesli ▶

Index

122

126